IMAGES
of America

MANSFIELD

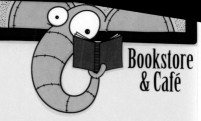

Bookstore & Café

A community gathering place to hang out, talk about books and meet amazing authors. We know you will feel right at home, and put our special events on your calendar.

111 South Street
Plainville, MA 02762
(508) 699-0244
www.AnUnlikelyStory.com

At An Unlikely Story
you will find...

- Great Books
- Unique Gifts
- Amazing Authors
- Healthy Fare
- Complimentary Gift Wrapping

Shop online anytime
www.AnUnlikelyStory.com

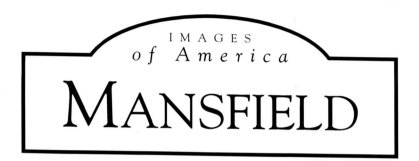

IMAGES
of America

MANSFIELD

Kevin B. McNatt
and Andrew J. Todesco

ARCADIA
PUBLISHING

Published by Arcadia Publishing
Charleston, South Carolina

Printed in the United States of America

Library of Congress Catalog Card Number: 98088252

For all general information contact Arcadia Publishing at:
Telephone 843-853-2070
Fax 843-853-0044
E-mail sales@arcadiapublishing.com
For customer service and orders:
Toll-Free 1-888-313-2665

Visit us on the Internet at www.arcadiapublishing.com

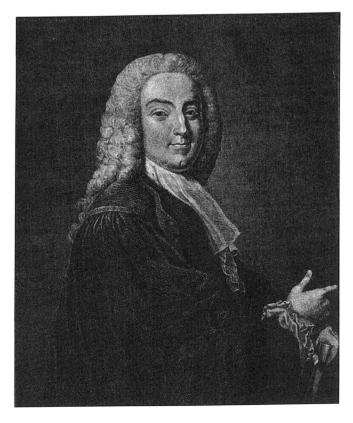

William Murray never set foot in Mansfield, Massachusetts, but the town was named after him. Murray, chief justice of England, was greatly admired by Massachusetts Royal Gov. Thomas Hutchinson. When Mansfield's petition to become a district arrived at the governor's desk in 1770, Hutchinson filled in the name "Mansfield" on the document to honor Murray, who had been elevated to the peerage of "Lord Mansfield."

CONTENTS

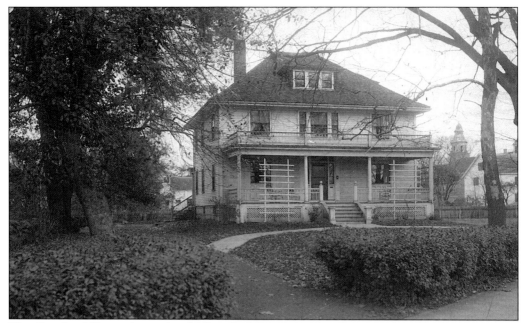

The Copeland House, located at 53 Rumford Avenue, is now home to the Mansfield Historical Society. Built in 1909, the house was a bequest to the Society from Jennie Copeland, the town's foremost historian, upon her death in 1956. The house contains artifacts and historical material from Mansfield's past, and is open to the public.

INTRODUCTION

Every city, town, and village is unique. That is what makes them interesting. The topic of this book is Mansfield, Massachusetts, a town we consider very unique. Originally a part of Taunton, then later set aside as the Norton North Precinct, Mansfield remained as such until 1770 when the region was incorporated as a district. In 1775, Mansfield achieved full legal status as a town. Mansfield came into being the same way hundreds of towns have over the years.

In many ways, Mansfield's history has followed a typical path. Originally very rural, farming was once its main occupation. Along the rivers sprang up small factories, many of which grew to be quite substantial. The Boston and Providence Railroad carved a path through Mansfield in 1835, making it a convenient location for the heavy industry that followed in the late 19th and early 20th centuries. Industry slowly declined, but the town became a haven for those looking for a pleasant little town in which to raise their children. So Mansfield remains today, a dot on the map, a nice place to live.

So what is it that makes Mansfield unique? That is a difficult question to answer. However, there has always been a certain sense and spirit that has set Mansfield aside from the rest. There were heroes and rascals, booms and busts, tragedies and triumphs. To write them all down and explain them would require thousands of pages. This book opts for a different approach.

A picture is worth a thousand words, the old saying goes. In this book are 231 photographs that we believe will show the reader what has made Mansfield unique. We have tried to let the pictures do as much of the talking as possible. In each caption, we have tried to identify the subject, give a few pertinent facts to orient the reader, and tell what happened to the subject. We trust that the pictures will do the rest.

We feel it is imperative that we explain the sources of our pictures. The majority of them are from the collection held by the Mansfield Historical Society. Others are courtesy of two venerable local institutions, the Mansfield Public Library and *The Mansfield News*, both of which allowed us free and open access to their collections. We would also like to specifically thank Lynn Holt and Bob Lanpher, both of whom allowed us to borrow from their collection of Mansfield postcards. We gratefully acknowledge the following individuals who loaned us photographs for this work: Diane Baldini, Janice Barrows, Ralph Bellavance, Angie Carbonetti, Anthony Farinella, Rita Hindman, Bob Lanpher, Jim McLaughlin, Dick Paulson, Steve Penesis, and Marion Wuschke. We also thank Saint Mary's Church for the use of their photographic archives. We would also note that some of the photographs came from town reports and souvenir programs from over the years. A note of thanks also goes to Doreen Tighe at Book Ends, for giving us the push to get started. In addition, thanks to Doreen and to Kristin Holster for proofreading.

We think that these photographs are interesting and a good representation of Mansfield's past. Hopefully this book will show the reader how much things have changed in Mansfield and how they have stayed the same in our unique little town.

One

AROUND THE
SOUTH COMMON

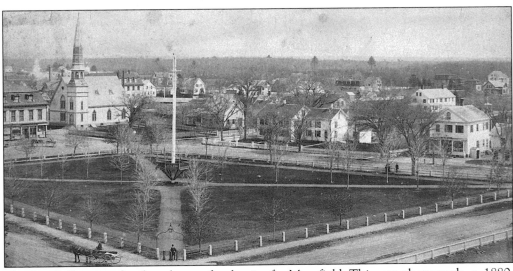

The South Common has long been a focal point for Mansfield. This rare photograph, c. 1880, shows the common similar to how we know it today. The intersection in the foreground, where the horse and buggy stand, is the corner of Union Street and Park Row. The building at the far left is the Lovell Block, which stands today. The building to the right is the Methodist church. There is an empty lot at the northeast corner of North Main and East Streets, where the Masonic Hall has long stood. The house on the adjacent side of the intersection was moved to 31 East Street in 1894, to make room for the home of S. Crocker Lovell. Other interesting observations include the gates over the entrances to the common, and the bandstand in the center. The photograph was taken from the belfry of the old meetinghouse on Union Street.

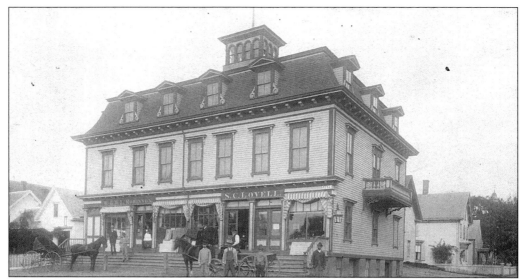

As we begin to look around the common, our first sight is the Lovell Block, which stands at the corner of North Main and West Streets. Built about 1870 by Isaac Lovell, it long housed the store of his brother S. Crocker Lovell. At the time, the building faced West Street, but the current address is 4 North Main Street. It is now widely known as George's Cleaners.

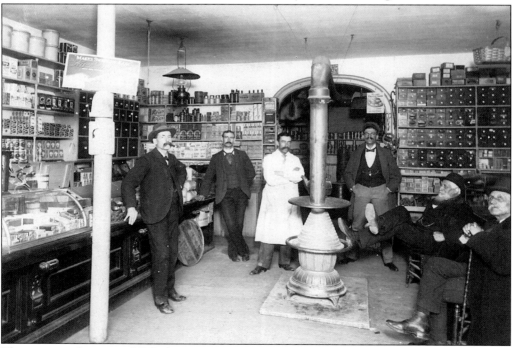

This group, relaxing in J.F. Robinson's grocery store in the Lovell Block, is engaged in one of Mansfield's favorite pastimes—talking! The man at the left is Jacob F. Robinson, the proprietor. Next we see his bookkeeper, Frank Knox, and clerks Charlie Aldrich and Willie Lovell (son of S. Crocker Lovell). Seated are longtime residents Jacob Blake and Ferdinand Cabot. The picture dates to the late 1890s or early 1900s.

10

This 1865 photograph shows Civil War veteran Samuel Crocker Lovell (1839–1918). Near the war's end, Lovell was chosen to escort Gen. Robert E. Lee through hostile Union lines after Lee's surrender at Appomattox. Once a safe distance away, Lee shook the lieutenant's hand and wished him "Godspeed and a safe return." Upon Lovell's return to Mansfield he opened a boot and shoe store and became one of the town's most-respected citizens.

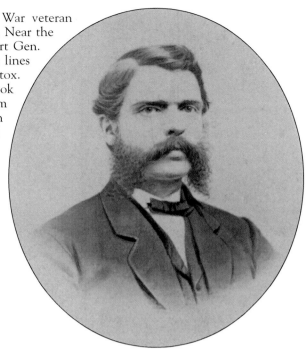

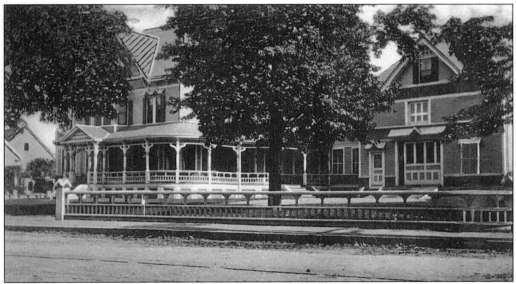

S. Crocker Lovell's house was located at the corner of South Main and East Streets. The Queen Anne-style home was built in 1894. Many still recall the elaborate fence that surrounded the Lovell property. This dignified structure stood at the location until 1965, when it was moved to 23 East Street to make room for a gas station.

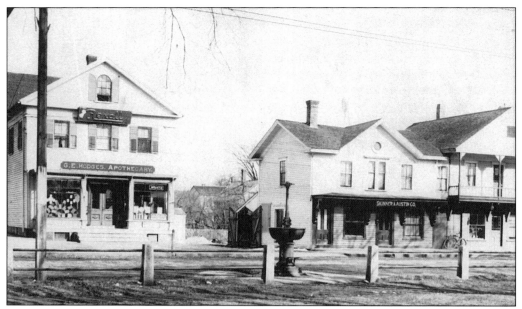

To the right of S. Crocker Lovell's home we would see this scene. At left is the drugstore of G.E. Hodges, whose present address would be 14 South Main Street. To the right is Skinner and Austin, a grocery store. The photograph was taken from the South Common, as the familiar granite posts and iron rails indicate. The contraption in the center is a water trough for horses. (Courtesy of the Mansfield Public Library.)

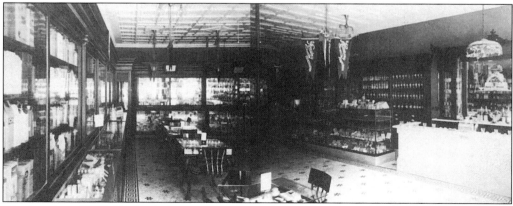

The interior of G.E. Hodges's drugstore was typical of its day. From this photograph we see that Mr. Hodges offered much more than prescriptions. Also for sale were chocolates, soft drinks, perfumes, cosmetics, and tobacco products. The tin ceiling and tile floor provide an additional touch from a bygone era.

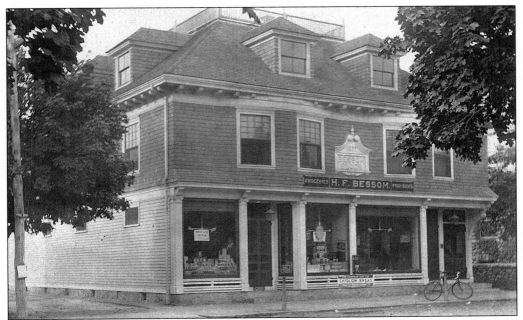

In the early 20th century, we would have seen the store of H.F. Bessom. Members of the Bessom family were proprietors of several successful stores in Mansfield. Henry Bessom's store was located on Park Row, facing the South Common. The building was located on the site of the Park Row School, which has recently been converted into the town hall.

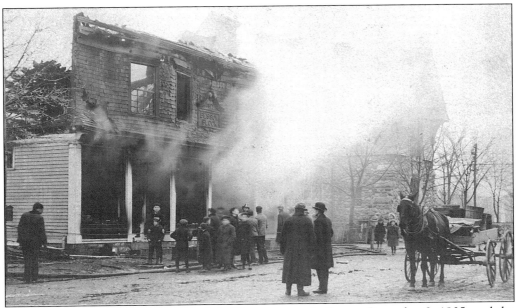

Sadly, the Bessom Block had a short life. The store caught fire on December 2, 1905, and the building was a total loss. By 1911, the town had purchased the lot and erected the school. One should take note of the building at the right, Memorial Hall.

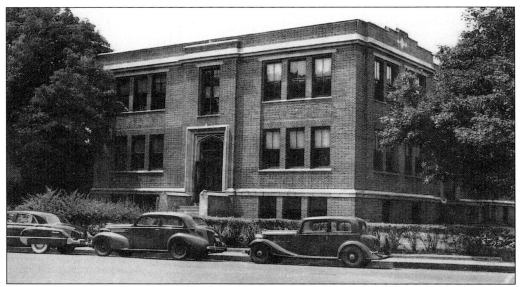

The town has long since got its money's worth out of this building. Constructed in 1911 at Park Row and South Main Street, Mansfield High School was considered a modern marvel. By 1954 the high school had relocated to East Street, but this building served elementary students as the Park Row School until 1992. Since 1997 the building has been the town hall.

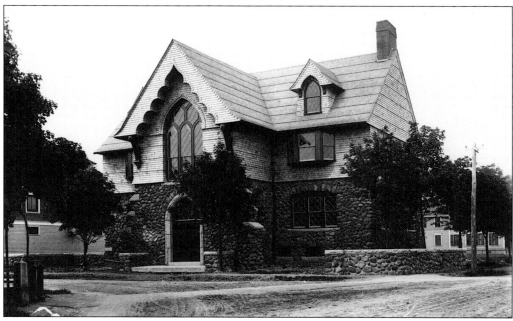

Memorial Hall now enjoys a spot on the National Register of Historic Places, but in this photograph from c. 1900, it was barely a year old. Dedicated in honor of Mansfield's Civil War veterans, the Victorian Gothic structure was used as a headquarters for Mansfield's chapter of the GAR, or Grand Army of the Republic. It was also home to the Mansfield Public Library until 1989. The town now uses this building at the corner of Park Row and Union Street as office space.

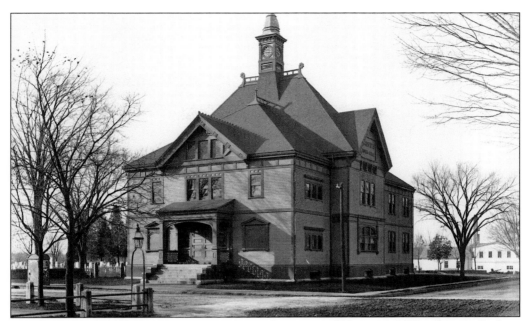

The stunning old town hall sat on a tiny lot at the corner of Union and West Streets. Built in 1883, it served as both the political and social hub of the town, hosting town offices as well as dances and many other functions. The South Common and the old town cemetery are at left, while one sees Packard's sawmill further down West Street on the right. Fire claimed the town hall on December 20, 1970, and the lot is now a memorial to Mansfield's war veterans.

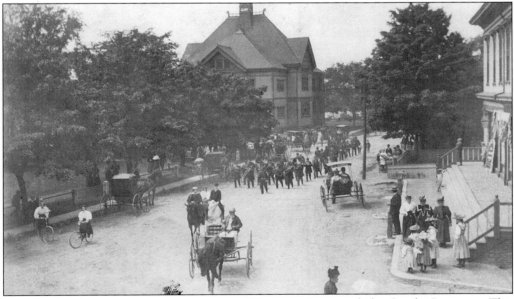

No Mansfield parade would be complete without a trip around the South Common. This undated photograph shows the marching band of Mansfield's GAR chapter proceeding past the South Common and the town hall at the left. To the right is a rare view of the staircase that served as an entryway to Lovell's Block, and shows that the front of the building once faced West Street.

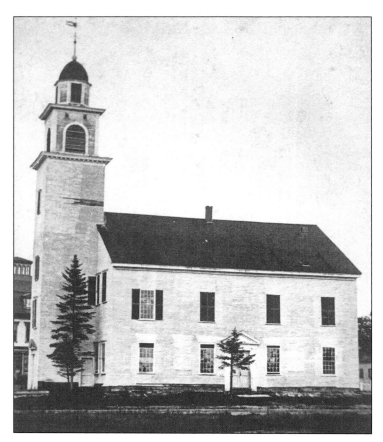

The old meetinghouse was built in 1766 and was the center of village political affairs as the line between church and state was indistinguishable in early New England. The building originally sat on the South Common, as this photograph from about 1870 indicates (note the Lovell Block in the background). In 1872 it was moved to a plot on Union Street next to the old cemetery, and was torn down in 1888. Our earlier panoramic photograph of the common was taken from its belfry.

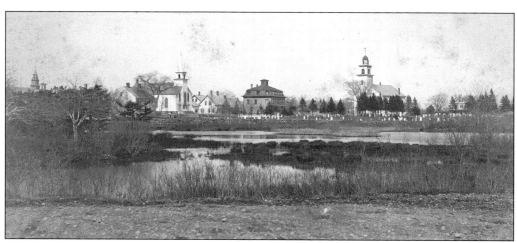

Our closing photograph of the South Common area, taken from across Kingman's Pond in 1870 or 1871, gives us a final overview. The tall steeple at the left belongs to the Baptist church. We can clearly see the Congregational church before it was remodeled, and beyond is Lovell's Block. The meetinghouse is still on the common with the old town cemetery in its foreground.

Two

MAIN STREET

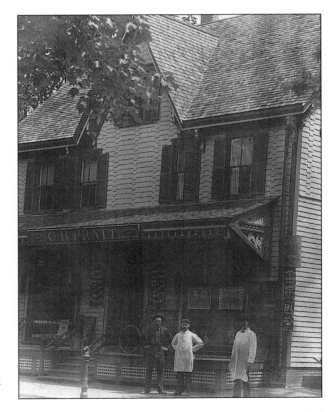

This remarkable photograph begins our tour of Main Street, certainly the most important thoroughfare in our town's history. Pictured here is the store of Charles H. Pratt, which was located at the corner of South Main Street and Wilson Place. The market was known to later generations as Filion's Market, then Findley's Market, until it was claimed by fire in the 1970s. From the residential South End, we will now move to the more commercial North Main Street.

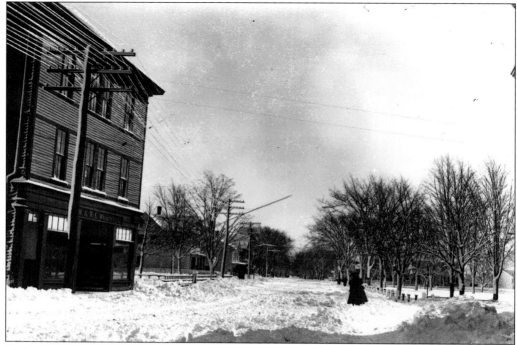

By the early 1890s William L. Robinson had established his dry goods store at the corner of North Main and East Streets, across from the Lovell Block and pictured here on the left. The building was known as the Masonic Block and is still located at 5 North Main Street. The woman at the center is walking towards the South Common through the barely passable snow-covered intersection of North and South Main Streets with East and West Streets, c. 1900.

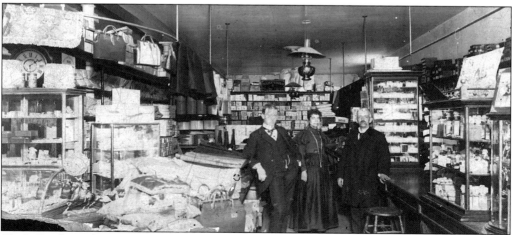

Clerk Frank Fairbanks of W.L. Robinson's dry goods store poses at left with fellow clerk Cora Bessom. At the right is Fairbanks's father, Henry Fairbanks, in a photograph showing about half the store as it appeared in the Masonic Block. Robinson's was established in 1878 in Lovell's Block and relocated in the early 1890s. The store should not be confused with Jacob Robinson's grocery store, also located in the Lovell Block after the dry goods store moved out.

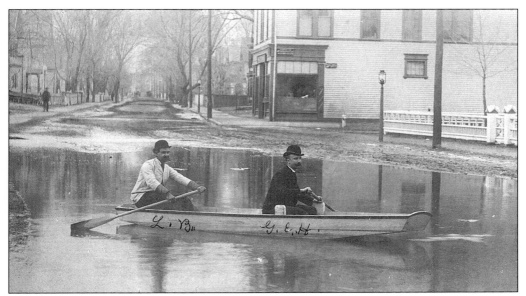

The Great Flood of 1886 provided Lewis Bessom, left, and George Hodges an opportunity to have some fun with a rowboat on South Main Street. Above Bessom is a view of North Main Street looking north, while above Hodges is the Masonic Block. At right is the fence surrounding S. Crocker Lovell's property. A wider shot would have revealed the South Common at the left.

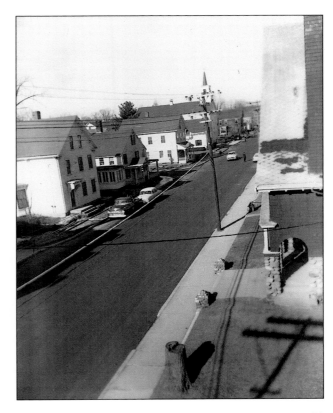

From atop the Masonic Block one would have seen this view of North Main Street in the late 1950s. The intersection of Fulton Street is visible on the left, and farther up is the steeple of the First Baptist Church. To the immediate right is the Methodist church, as it still appears today. (Courtesy of *The Mansfield News*.)

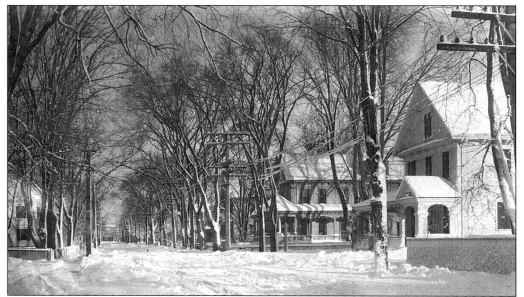

This undated view of North Main Street at the intersection of Park Street shows the front of the beautiful home that sat on the southeast corner and has since burned down. One building farther north shows the familiar verandah of Sherman's Funeral Home at 55 North Main Street, still known to Mansfield residents today.

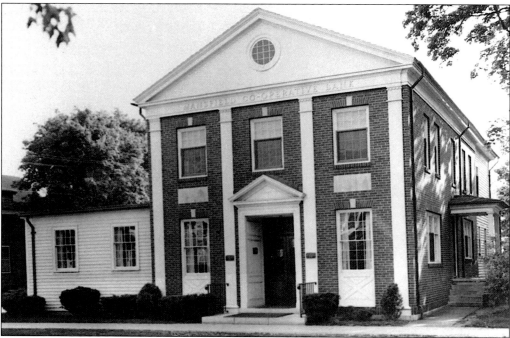

Founded in 1883, the Mansfield Cooperative Bank is a longtime Main Street institution. In 1950, the bank moved to this location, the former home of Rev. Jacob Ide. The building, demolished in 1987, sat in what is now the bank's parking lot to the right of its current 80 North Main Street home. (Courtesy of *The Mansfield News*.)

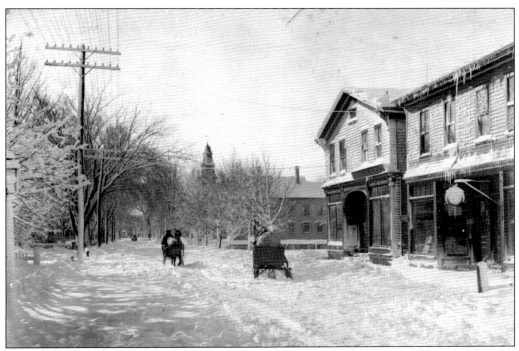

A snow-covered but busy North Main Street is our next subject. The high steeple down the road belongs to the First Baptist Church, while the house with six windows visible belonged to Rev. Jacob Ide. The facade with the archway was the studio of Mansfield photographer J. Ralph Allen. The photograph is undated, but it is probably from the early 1900s. (Courtesy of the Mansfield Public Library.)

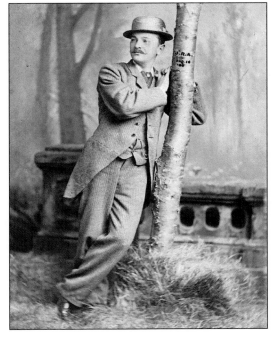

This dashing figure is none other than the legendary Mansfield photographer J. Ralph Allen, then just 23 years old. Allen arrived from Rhode Island in 1882, and had his studio in the above Foster Block location by 1890. Remaining in Mansfield until his death in 1912, Allen was a great practical joker, an ardent tennis player, and known to be "graceful on the roller skates."

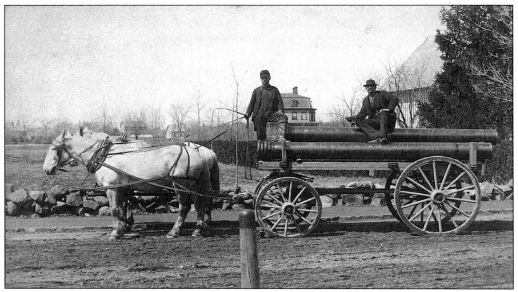

These workmen are laying down pipes on North Main Street for Mansfield's first water system, completed at a cost of $67,459. The house located behind the two workers stands today at 86 Rumford Avenue, and the other buildings were on High Street. Much of Main Street and Rumford Avenue was yet to be developed in this photograph from April 1888.

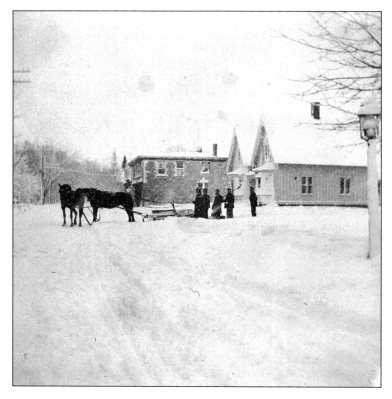

Snow always made traveling difficult, and this crew at the corner of Villa and North Main Streets are working to clear the road. The twin-peaked building at the right is 126 North Main, now the home of Eames Insurance. The buildings farther down, at 108 and 114 North Main, are also recognizable landmarks today. Note the kerosene lamp in the immediate right foreground.

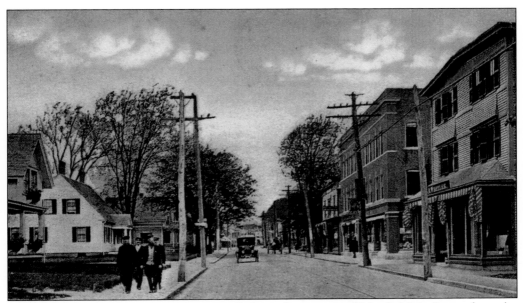

Mansfieldians of today can recognize much from this picture of North Main Street from the 1920s. This time we are looking north at the corner of Villa Street. The three clearly visible buildings on the right are still landmarks today. First is 121 North Main Street, now O'Malley Real Estate. Next is the Wheeler Building at 129 North Main, currently True Value Hardware. The third is 141 North Main Street, which is now Jimmy's Pub. Opposite the Wheeler Building is a private home, where now stands the brick building pictured below.

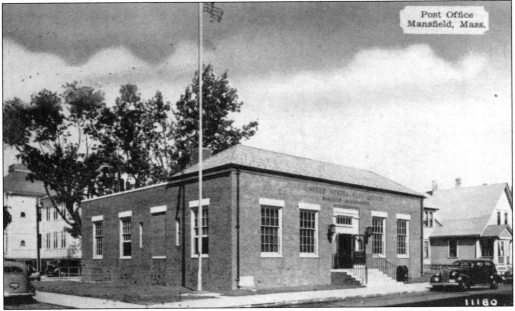

To get Americans back to work, the government constructed many public buildings during the Great Depression. One was Mansfield's Post Office, which was built in 1937. It served as the post office until the relocation to Giles Place. The building remains today at North Main and Villa Streets, now home to the Elks Club. In back, take note of the Central School.

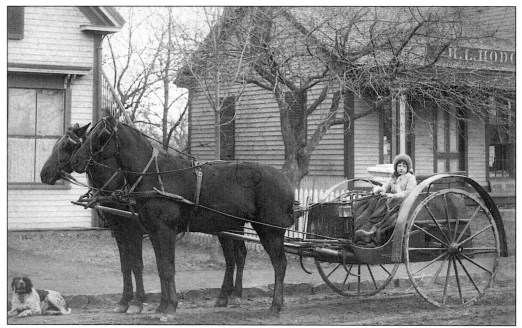

This photograph, c. 1890, shows young Beulah Bailey with horses Topey and Dick and her dog, Bessie. They are in front of the North Main Street shop of Hannah L. Hodges, a milliner located near Villa Street. There is a sign on the milliner's front porch reading "patterns."

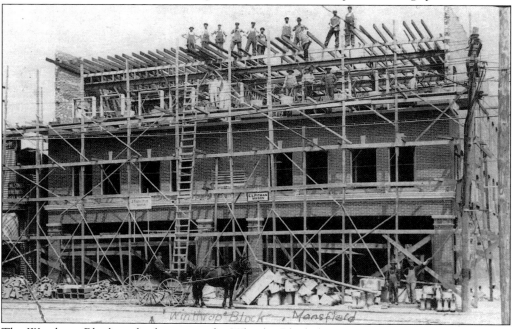

The Winthrop Block, today known as the Wheeler Block, has stood at 129 North Main Street since this construction began in 1903. The posted signs indicate that longtime Mansfield builder James Findlater was the contractor, and E.L. Pitman was the mason. The imposing brick facade still stands out on Main Street today.

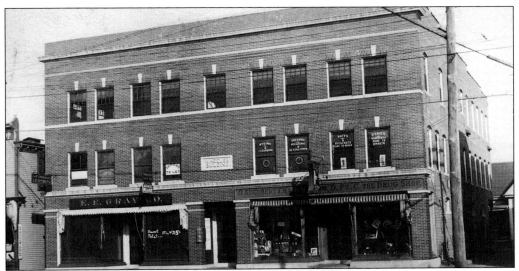

And this is how the Wheeler block appeared when finished. This view, from c. 1917, shows the grocery store of E.E. Gray at ground level, which later was home to the Central Market. Next door is the drug shop of G. Adelbert Emard, which would become the well-known Lilly's Drugstore. On the second floor were professional offices, including Dentists W.T. and R.W. Dickerman shown here. The town used the offices in the interim after the town hall fire of 1970. And the Odd Fellows used the top floor as their meetingplace for several decades.

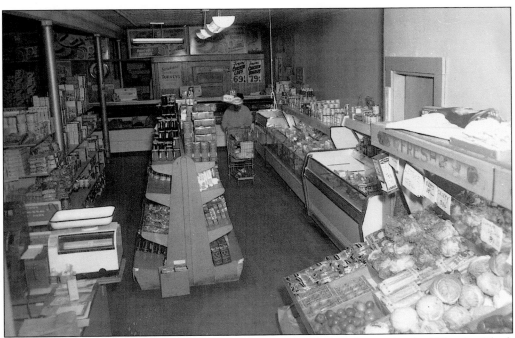

This is the interior of the Central Market, operated by Angelo Linari in the Wheeler Block for many years, as it appeared in the late 1950s. It was later sold and became associated with the I.G.A. chain of supermarkets, and was then moved to the commercial building where the former Central School was located on Villa Street. (Courtesy of *The Mansfield News*.)

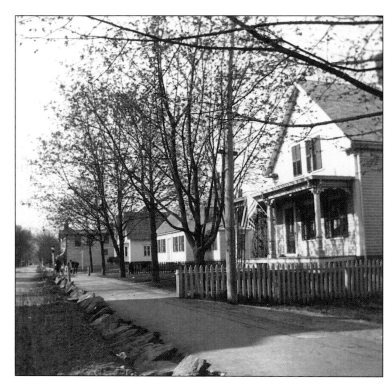

The home of Frank W. Copeland, at right, is another North Main Street mainstay. Located at 150 North Main Street, later generations would know it as the home of Dr. John Cook. Today's residents know it as RIM Engineering. Other interesting features of this southerly view include the stone curbing on the unpaved roadway, and the presence of many trees along Main Street.

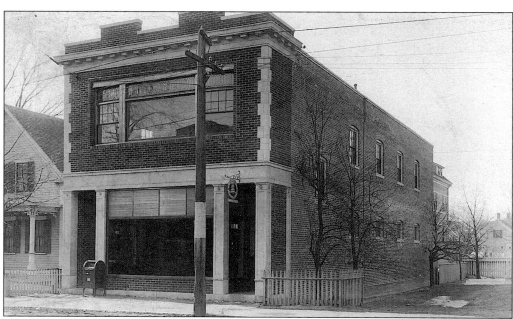

One hundred sixty-two North Main Street has served many purposes over the years. The building housed the post office from 1914 to 1938. Upstairs was the phone company's switchboard for Mansfield, where operators transferred phone calls manually until Mansfield garnered dial service in 1957. Other than its occupants, the building is essentially unchanged today.

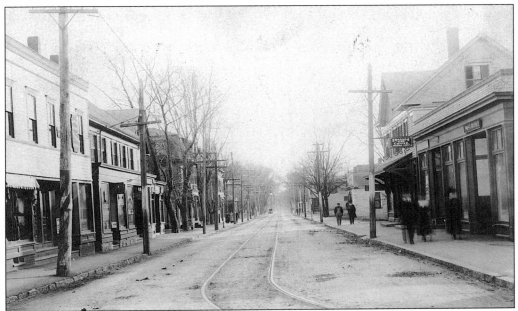

Cars were much more of a rarity on North Main Street in the early 20th century, when this photograph was taken at the corner of High Street. One lone automobile can be spotted well down on the left. However, a keen observer would note the trolley track running down the road. One could travel to Easton, Foxboro, and Norton by trolley at the time, and then on to the larger cities like Attleboro, Taunton, or Brockton.

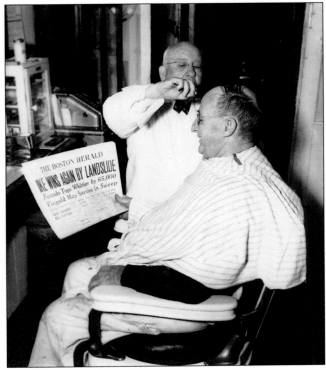

Another genuine Main Street institution was George Sawyer, a barber for six decades. A staunch democrat, Sawyer had to give a year's worth of free haircuts to Frank Devine after Sawyer's 1956 presidential candidate, Adlai Stevenson, lost to Devine's choice, President Eisenhower. Devine grins at *The Boston Herald*, which cries "Ike Wins Again By Landslide." Sawyer lost the same bet to Devine in 1952. Sawyer's shop was located in the Fox Block just north of 141 North Main Street, and is now demolished. (Photograph courtesy of *The Mansfield News*.)

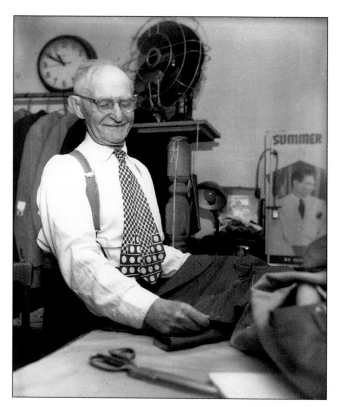

Just up the road from George Sawyer we would have found local tailor Ezra Syat. Mr. Syat's shop was located in the building that some Mansfieldians call "The Flatiron Building," due to its similar shape to the well-known Flatiron Building in New York City. (Ours, however, is considerably smaller!) The building's current address is 191 North Main Street.

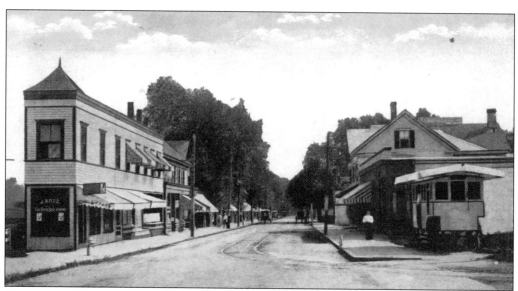

Here at the left we see the Flatiron Building in this view of Main Street from the corner of High Street. Kingsley's Diner stood across the street from the building, in front of which ran the trolley tracks on their way to Rumford Avenue and on to the train depot. The trolley tracks were built on High Street because they were not allowed to cross the train tracks just ahead.

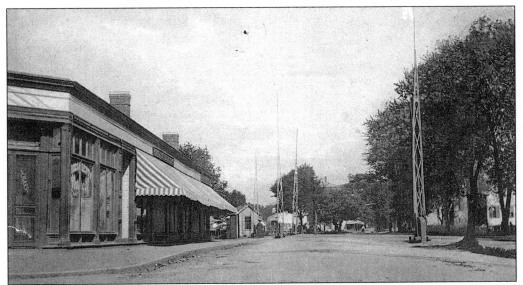

And here are those train tracks as we look at Main and High Streets, but this time looking north. The building at the left still stands at this location, but gone are the Old Colony Line railroad tracks that crossed the road from 1836 to 1956. A guard located in the small shack pictured here lowered the gates to stop road traffic while trains on their way to and from Taunton passed.

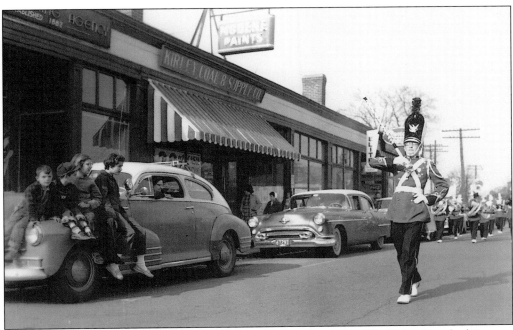

Soon after the tracks were removed, the stretch of the former railroad bed from Rumford Avenue to Main Street became Old Colony Road. That is the direction that drum major George Upper and the Mansfield High School Marching Band are proceeding from as they pass the Herbert E. King Insurance Agency and Kirley Coal & Supply at 212 North Main Street in this 1956 parade. (Courtesy of *The Mansfield News*.)

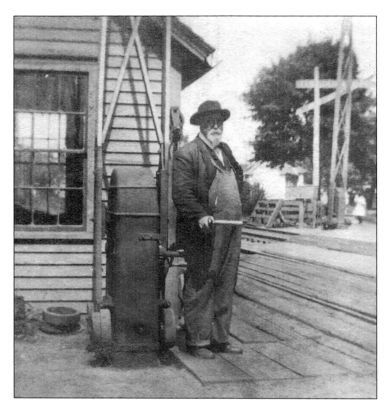

Before the underpasses, dead-end streets, and abandoned railroad beds of today, Mansfield had several busy grade crossings that the trains would pass over. Here we see gate-tender Warren Skinner at his post where the Old Colony Line crossed North Main Street. Gate tenders would lower the gates as a train went through so road traffic would not collide with the trains.

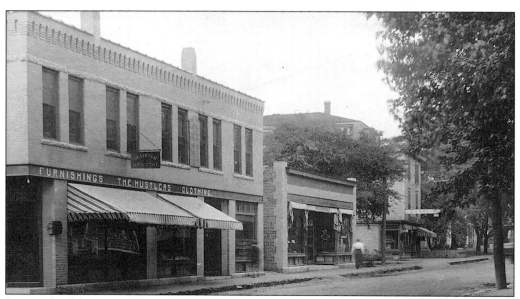

Just north of the Main Street grade crossing we'd find this scene, still recognizable today. At the left we see 234 North Main, which backs up to Old Colony Road. The next building remains, and just beyond that is W.L. Stearns, where it has been located for over 125 years.

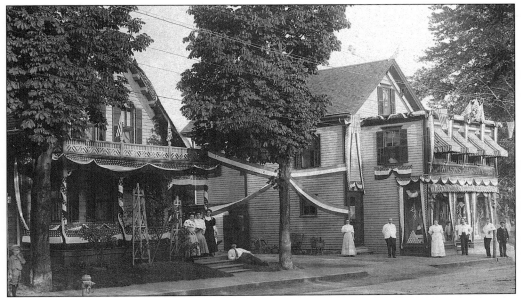

Across the street from our previous shot we'd have found this scene, probably taken at the 1907 Old Home Week celebration. The house at the left is no more, but once sat at North Main and Cottage Streets. The location is now 247 North Main Street, home of the Cheng Du Restaurant and Linda Jodice Salon. The building at the right still stands at 243 North Main, and at the time was Wilson's Pharmacy.

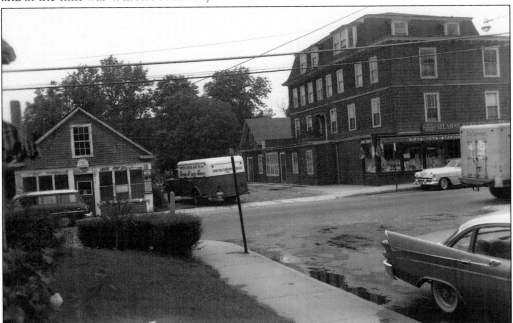

This photograph from the 1950s looks back at North Main from Cottage Street. W.L. Stearns is a recognizable landmark, in the same location at 262 North Main Street since 1873. The building at the left is gone, but at the time was most likely still George's Cleaners before the business relocated to the South Common. (Courtesy of *The Mansfield News*.)

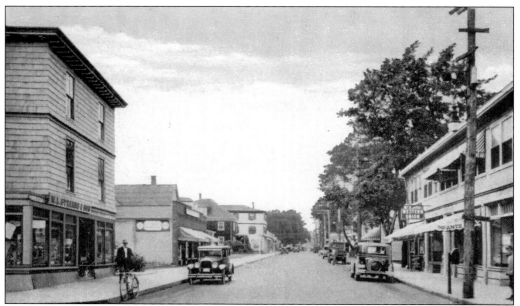

Contractor and builder David M. Eddy built the block at the far right around 1920, at the corner of Cottage Street. The Eddy Block at 267 North Main Street still bears his name. This view of the street looking north bears several still-familiar landmarks.

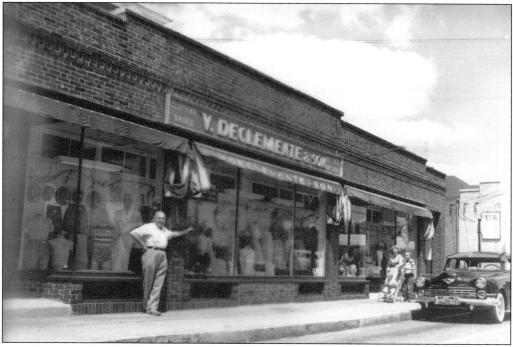

Vincent DeClemente operated his department store from the building pictured here at 272 North Main Street. This photograph was taken in 1956, when DeClemente's was celebrating its 40th anniversary in Mansfield. (Courtesy of *The Mansfield News*.)

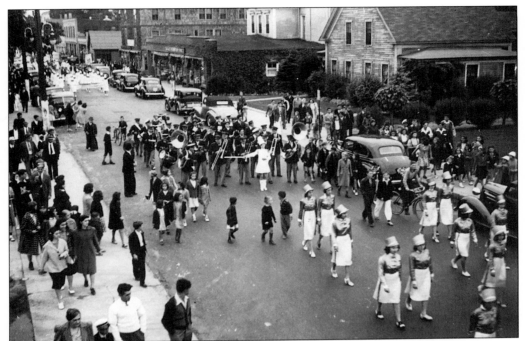

This photograph was taken on July 4, 1940, and provides another view of North Main Street. Visible down the road are 234 North Main, followed by the small store that was then probably George's Cleaners. Next is W.L. Stearns's, then DeClemente's, followed by a private home that is now demolished. In its place is the commercial building at 284 North Main.

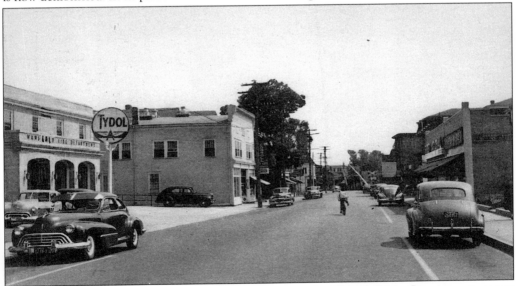

Newcomers to Mansfield may not recall when this stretch of North Main Street saw two-way traffic. At left, on the corner of Pleasant Street, sat a Tydol gas station. Also at the left of the photograph are the central fire station, then the office and apartment building at 277 North Main Street, across from DeClemente's. The boy on the bike had considerably less traffic to worry about then!

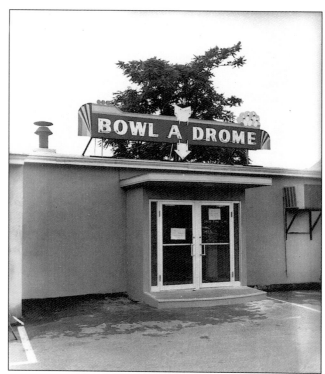

The Mansfield Bowl-A-Drome was located in what is now the parking lot next to the former Sannie's block. One could gain entrance to the parking lot from Main Street or Old Colony Road. The former roller skating rink was remodeled as a bowling alley in 1956.

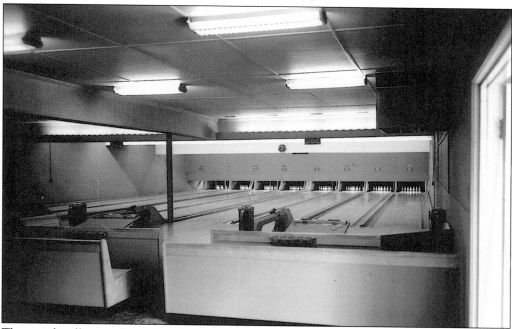

These eight alleys made up the playing area at the Bowl-A-Drome. As a customer entered the building, he would have seen the alleys on the right. To the left, closer to North Main Street, was Club Daggs, a lounge that made an evening's entertainment complete. The building has since been demolished.

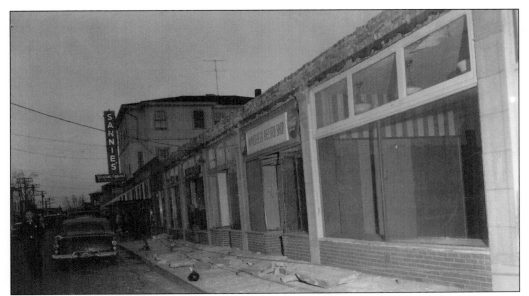

Tragedy was barely averted on November 27, 1957, when the cast stone above the Wasserman Block unexpectedly fell to the ground at 3:30 p.m. Shortly thereafter, the entire block was purchased by Sannie's, the longtime Main Street clothing store. The Sannie's sign that we see here became a Mansfield landmark for decades. (Courtesy of *The Mansfield News*.)

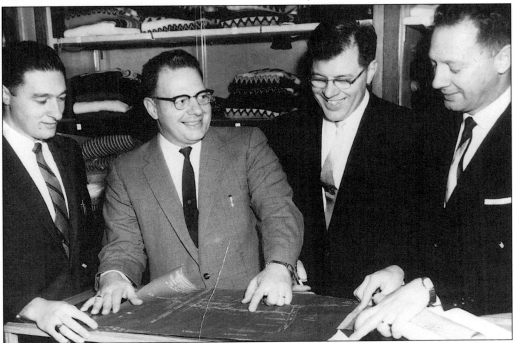

The Farinella Brothers owned and operated Sannie's Inc. Here are the corporation's officers as they prepare to expand the store in 1958: Charlie Farinella, vice president; Sannie Farinella, president; Frank Farinella, secretary/clerk; and Tony Farinella, treasurer. Sannie's store remained at the corner of North Main and Thomas Streets until it closed in 1992.

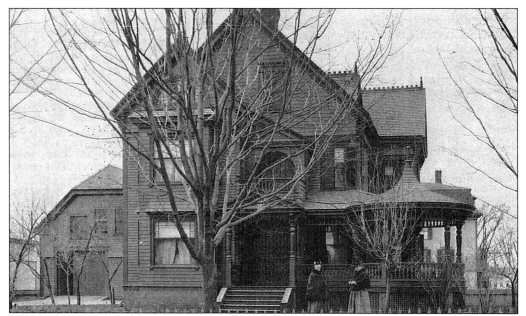

The home of jewelry-manufacturer Doliver Spaulding stood on the corner of North Main and Chauncy (now Thomas) Streets. The elegant home had a large carriage house, seen here at the rear, and an elaborate porch that is now gone. The home was later moved slightly to the west, farther up on Thomas Street.

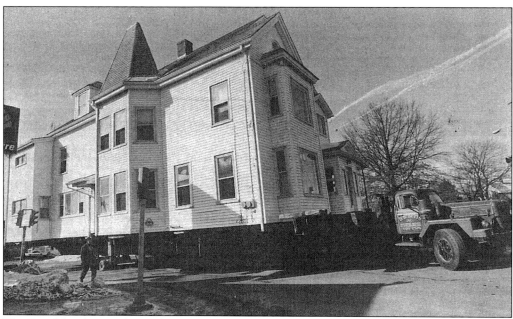

The Spaulding house changed hands a few times but remained at its new Thomas Street location until January 21, 1994. The Friday afternoon bustle of Route 106 stood still that day to allow the mammoth house to make its way to another new location, 80 Pratt Street. Hundreds of interested observers lined the sidewalks to watch the giant creep down the roadway.

Three

THE NORTH END

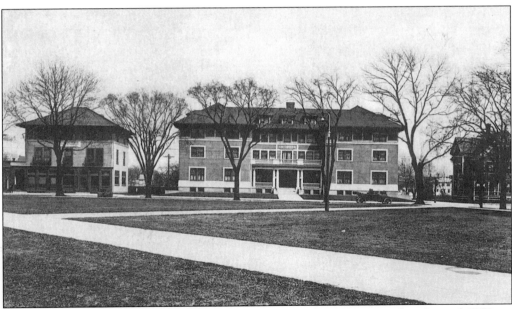

The North Common, as it existed before the underpasses were constructed in the mid-1950s, is now just a memory. The construction took half of the North Common, as the Chauncy Street underpass now claims almost up to the point where the two concrete walks meet. The large building in the center was Walter Lowney's elegant hotel, "The Tavern." An extension of Route 106 was constructed at the same time through the former Tavern property, rerouting the state highway to form a straight connection to where 106 continues on Pratt Street. Formerly, those traveling Route 106 eastbound drove up Chauncy, then took a left on to North Main Street, and a right on to Pratt Street.

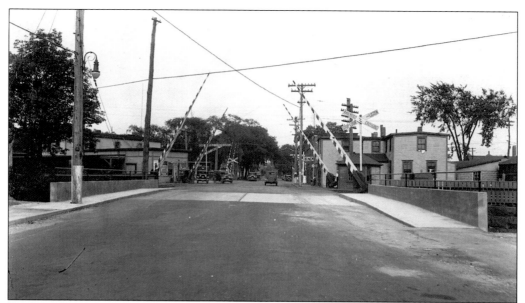

Eastbound travelers on Chauncy Street once crossed this bridge over the Rumford River. This scene from 1933 shows that the travelers had to contend with two railroad crossings—the first was the main line from Boston to Providence, and the second was the Old Colony Line. To the left is the old depot building.

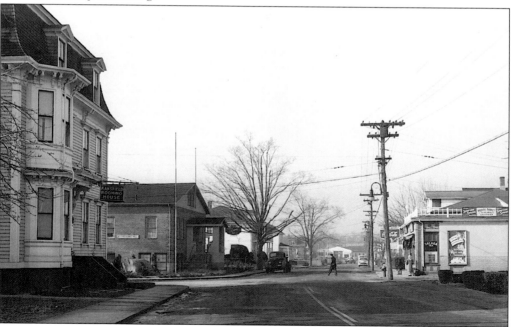

How did westbound travelers get to the North End? By Pratt Street, of course, and this 1950 photograph shows the route. At left are the Mansfield Rooming House and the original Gloria Columbo Hall, which were on the intersection of Pratt Street and Chilson Avenue. All buildings on the left were demolished to make way for the Chauncy Street extension of Route 106. Also now gone is Pagnini's Market, which we see on the right.

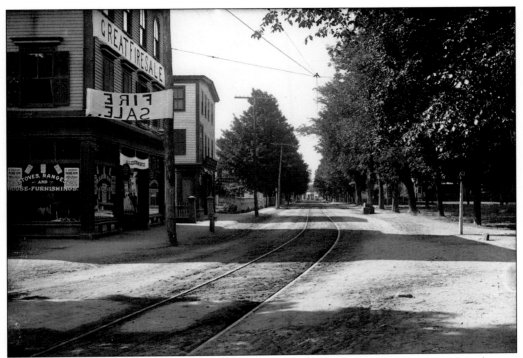

And, if you were coming into town from the North End by North Main Street in 1900, here is what you would have seen. Hayhurst's store and the First National Bank were on the left. The North Common, also known as Lowney Park, was on the right. The trolley tracks ran from Mansfield's depot through the Back Bay section of town and on to Easton.

Gardner Chilson's home was located on the property later occupied by The Tavern. In 1907, Walter Lowney moved it one plot north to build his hotel. Chilson's home was remodeled into the First National Bank building. It has taken several incarnations over the years, and though greatly remodeled, the first floor remains today as the BankBoston at 355 North Main Street.

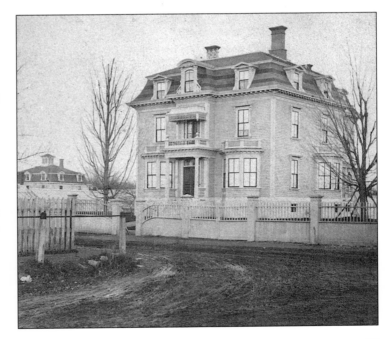

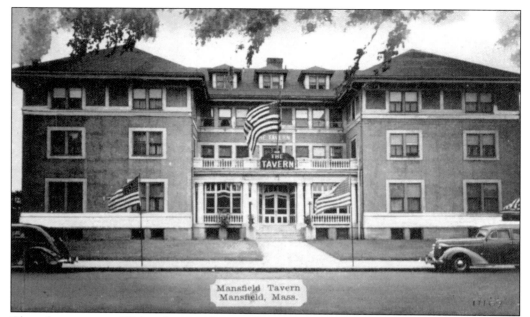

Mansfield Tavern
Mansfield, Mass.

Chocolate-magnate Walter Lowney began The Tavern in 1907 and completed it in 1909 at the whopping cost of $350,000. It was called "a roadside Waldorf," and was built as Lowney's luxurious winter home as well as a hotel. After Lowney's death in 1921, the building changed hands several times and fell into disrepair. On July 31, 1948, the stately building caught fire, and the remains were torn down in June 1950. Route 106 now travels through the property.

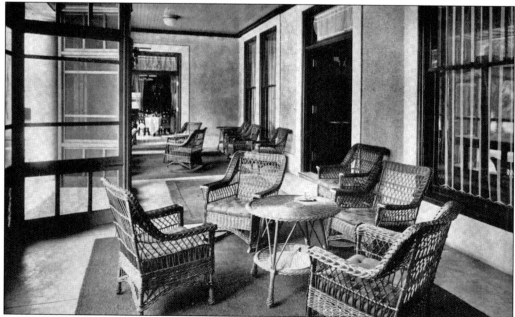

The Tavern's breezy front porch provided guests a comfortable and relaxing spot from which to observe the bustle of Main Street. One could also consider the generosity of Walter Lowney, who fixed up the unsightly land in the front and donated it to the town as the North Common.

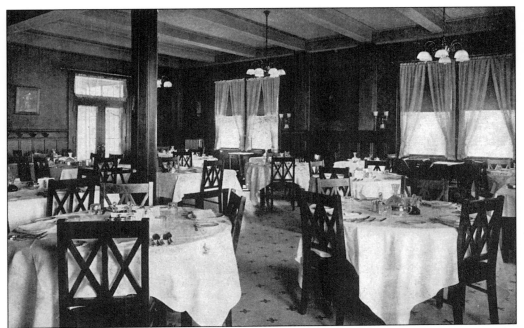

The Tavern's dining room shows Lowney's desire for a first-class establishment, as well as the decadence of the "Gilded Age," during which it was built. The Tavern earned an outstanding reputation for fine dining.

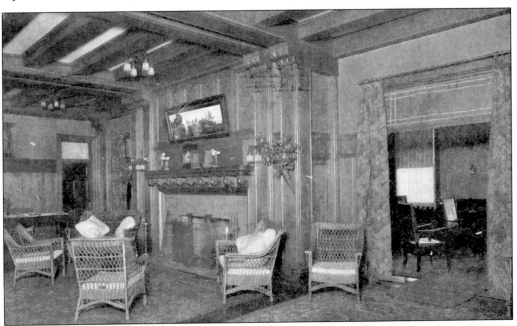

Cigars, brandy, and conversation were probably the perfect after-dinner accompaniment at The Tavern on most nights. And, where else were they best enjoyed but here in this beautiful parlor? This picture provides a glimpse of an elegant age that touched even small towns like Mansfield.

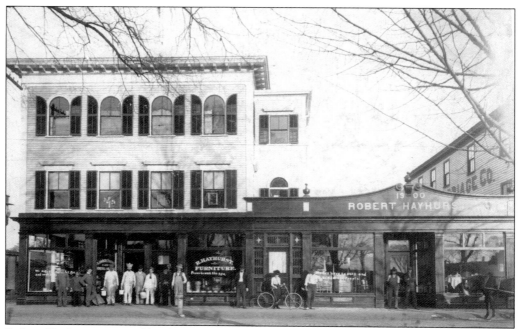

Robert Hayhurst operated his furniture store from this building in the early 1900s. Though now only two stories high, the building still stands at 363 North Main Street across from the North Common. Today we know it as Grogan-Marciano Sporting Goods.

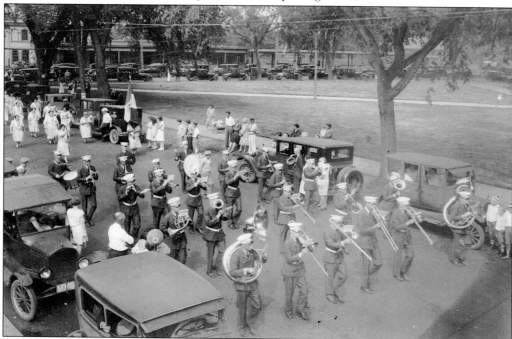

This merry band is making its way around the North Common as it once appeared. The parade is proceeding east on Chauncy Street. The building visible in the background is the old depot, torn down in 1952 and located near the sight of the present depot.

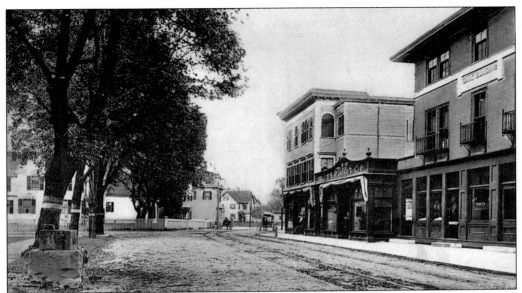

Here's North Main Street looking north in front of the common. At the immediate right is the "Bank Building," which long housed the First National Bank. More recently it has been Baybank, and is now BankBoston, with the top floors removed and the bottom floor greatly remodeled. W.C. Fuller's is one building north.

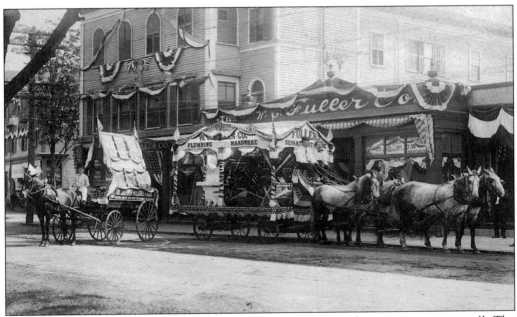

The W.C. Fuller Company sold hardware, furniture, and was a department store as well. The Fuller family took the block over from Robert Hayhurst around 1905. This photograph was taken during the Old Home Week celebration of 1907, where Fullers contributed these horse-drawn floats to the parade.

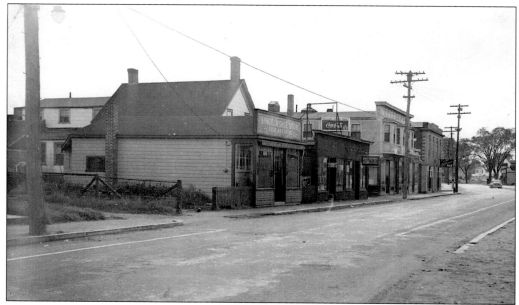

Just down the road from the North Common was the stretch of North Main Street that some called "Booze Boulevard," and for good reason. The first building pictured here is the Lincoln Shoe Store, but next were three bar rooms: The Club 433, The Mazzini Club, and Jack's Cafe (at the corner of Pratt and North Main). Across the street were The Regent, The Hi-Lo Club, and the Marconi Club. Whistles were also wetted nearby at the Mansfield House, the Gloria Columbo Hall, and the Club Seven (later Daggs). The photograph is c. 1940s.

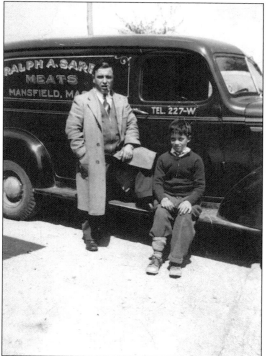

Sarro's Market is a North End mainstay even today, but this photograph from 1939 reflects a different era. Here we see the store's founder, Ralph Sarro, in front of his delivery truck, before he owned the store at 457 North Main Street. Mr. Sarro would peddle his wares directly from his truck. With Mr. Sarro is his young brother-in-law, Louis Narciso.

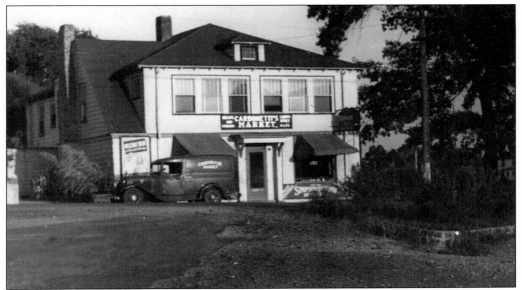

Carbonetti's Market was located at 525 North Main Street, on the corner of Angell Street. Opened for business in 1926 by Charles Carbonetti, the store sold meats and provisions. After Prohibition, Carbonetti's added a full line of wines and liquors for the convenience of its customers.

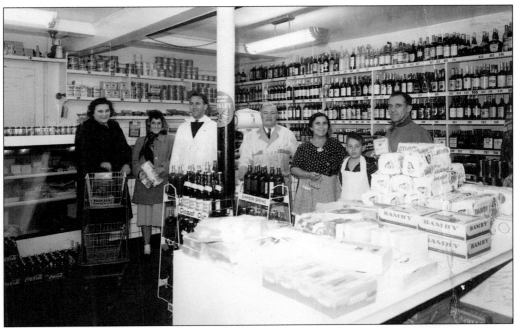

Here is the interior of Carbonetti's Market. From left to right are the following: Louise Soldani, Eleanor Palladino, Hugo Carbonetti, store founder Charles Carbonetti, his wife, Olivia Carbonetti, Albert Minucci, and Aldo Carbonetti. Charles Carbonetti ran the store until his death in 1953, when his son Hugo took over. The market closed in May 1971, and is now an apartment building.

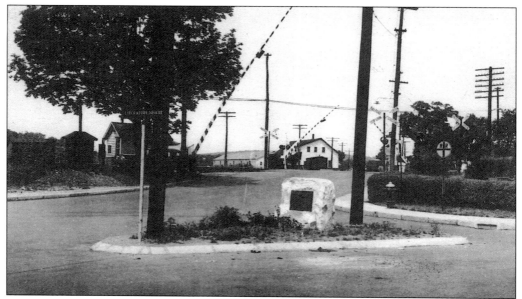

Liberatore Square was dedicated to the memory of the three Liberatore brothers, Guido, Wilfred, and John, all of whom were killed in action in World War II. Behind the square is the old North Main Street grade crossing for the Boston and Providence line. The building just beyond that was the freight house. The view looks north towards Foxboro.

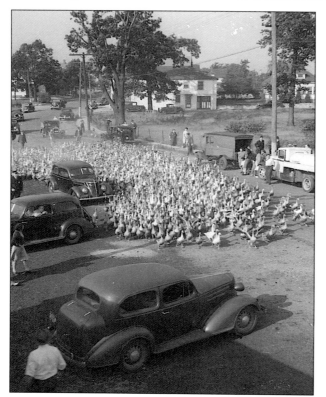

The annual parade of geese was a great Mansfield tradition for decades. The geese, arriving by train from Canada, were unloaded at the freight house (which would be at left in a wider shot) and marched to the Austin Goose Farm on Winter Street. The geese are marching down North Main towards Pratt Street, and the building at the above center is Carbonetti's Market.

Four

TRAINS, TROLLEYS, AND UNDERPASSES

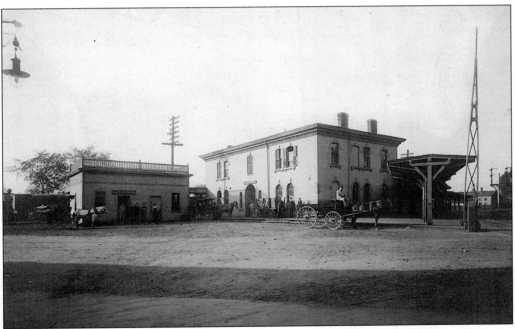

When the Boston and Providence Railroad was constructed through Mansfield in 1835, the town was changed forever. The town became a key location for New England railroading, the location where the main line sprouted two important branches—the Old Colony Railroad, which ran to Taunton and points south, and the Mansfield and Framingham Railroad, which ran to that town and points north. This photograph shows the old Mansfield depot, which sat near our current depot on the North Common. Earl and Prew's Express Office is at the left, and the Chilson Foundry (later Clemmey Tank) is visible at the right.

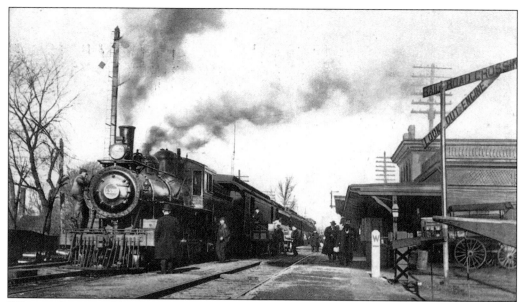

"This is where you'd land if you came to Mansfield," so wrote the author of a 1910 postcard with this photograph on the front. At the time, Mansfield's station hummed with industry and busy travelers. In a changed society, today it sees mostly commuters coming to and from Boston.

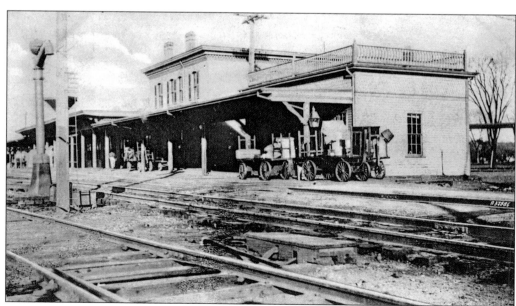

The old depot, constructed in 1860, served for almost a century. It slowly fell into disrepair, and was torn down in the summer of 1952. Soon after, a "temporary" station rose in its place—the same tiny barn-like structure familiar to Mansfieldians today, some 45 years later!

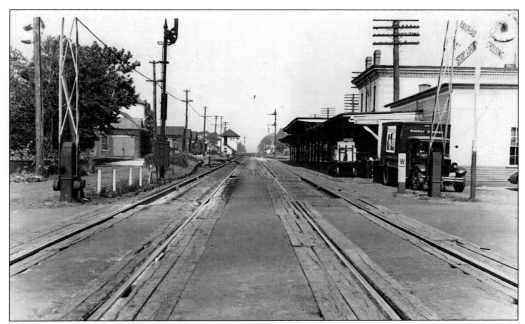

The railroad changed Mansfield in many ways. This view of the main line looking north towards Boston c. 1938 might remind us of the industry that sprang up around the railroad. We can see the old depot at right, and on the left side of the tracks was the former Chilson Foundry, then known as Clemmey Tank. As we will see in chapter six, Mansfield became an impressive industrial center for a town of its size, due in no small part to railroad accessibility.

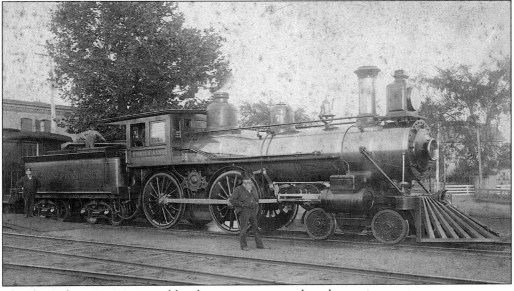

The days of majestic engines like this are now gone, but the engines were once a common sight in Mansfield. Here is Mansfield station agent Fred Paine standing in front of his massive namesake locomotive, c. 1888. The engine was built by the Taunton Locomotive Works, but the photograph was taken in Mansfield, as proven by the presence of the old depot in the left background.

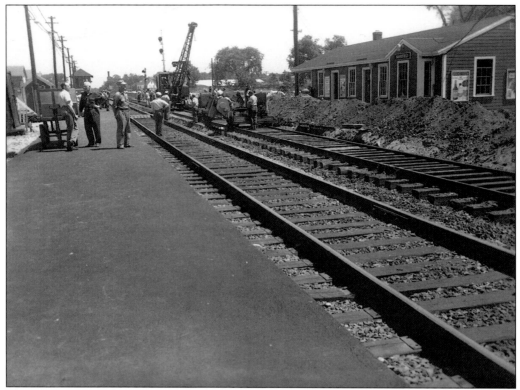

This modern view, from the late 1950s, shows the station area as we know it today. In the upper right is our "temporary" station that is still in use. An interesting observation is the signal tower above the men on the left that is now gone. (Courtesy of *The Mansfield News*.)

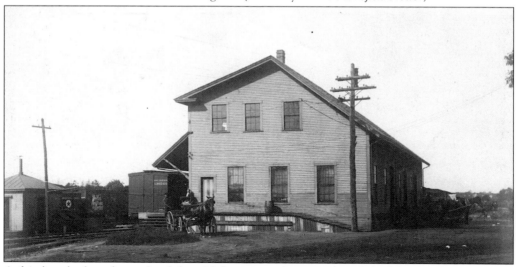

A few hundred yards north of the old depot was this now-demolished landmark, the freight house. The house was located along the tracks, next to the intersection of North Main and County Streets. The house was once a hive of activity, the place where all types of cargo was loaded and unloaded as it made its way to and from Mansfield.

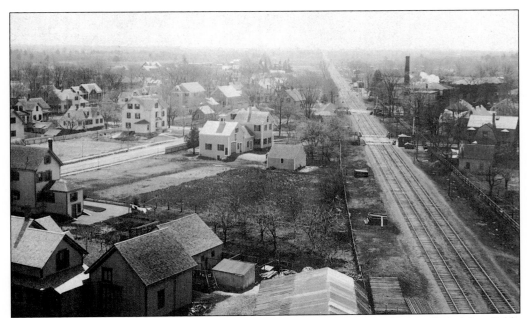

The Old Colony Railroad was constructed in 1836 and ran in a straight line from Mansfield's depot south through Norton and on to Taunton. This photograph, taken from atop the old grain mill looking south, shows three grade crossings—first Court Street, then Park Street, then East Street. The line was abandoned from the depot to North Main Street in 1956, but the stretch from the grain mill to Taunton remained open until 1965. The empty bed still remains today. The road at the left is Columbus Avenue, a part of the residential Back Bay section of town.

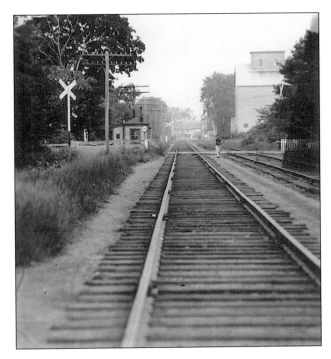

Here is the same stretch of tracks looking back toward Mansfield center. The grade crossing is Court Street and at the right is the grain mill, now an apartment complex. Longtime residents have bitter-sweet memories of waving to servicemen as their troop trains passed through Mansfield on their way to and from Camp Miles Standish in Taunton during WW II.

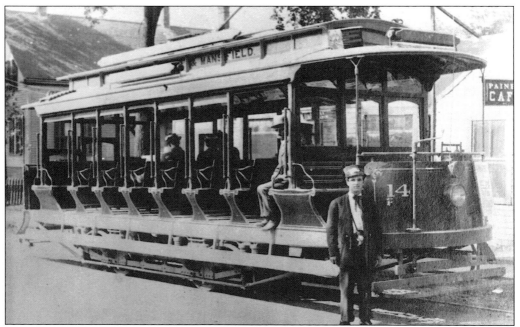

The 1890s to the 1920s saw the rise and demise of trolley lines in the area. This early trolley was open and subject to the elements, and was probably only used in the summer. This photograph was taken in front of Paine's Cafe, operated by station agent Fred Paine in the Mansfield depot. This line ran to Norton, and operated for nearly 30 years until it closed in 1928.

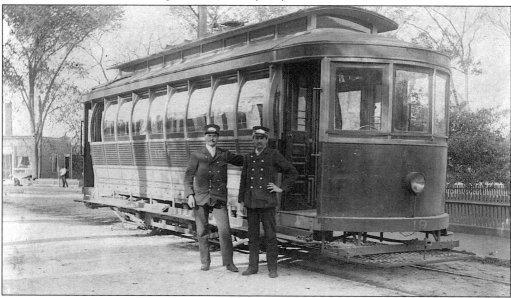

Trolley men Dan Johnston and George Matatall stand in front of this car, which belonged to the Easton line. The route was from the North Common to North Main Street, Pratt Street, Chilson Avenue, Samoset Avenue, Hodges Street, Court Street, through the Car Barn to Park Street, East Street, through East Mansfield, and on to Easton. The Easton Line was abandoned in 1908 due to a lack of riders. (Courtesy of the Mansfield Public Library.)

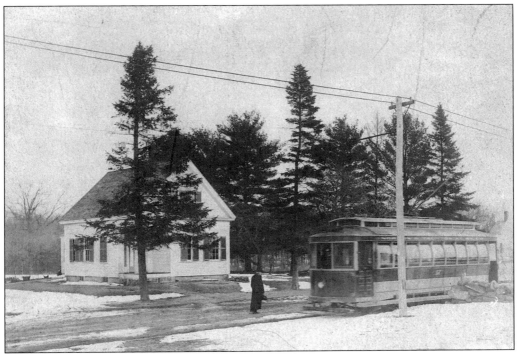

The Reverend Ephraim A. Hunt of the Methodist church of East Mansfield watches the trolley pass by his parsonage in 1907. This car was equipped with pull-down hatches that could be raised in good weather and closed to keep out rain, snow, and cold.

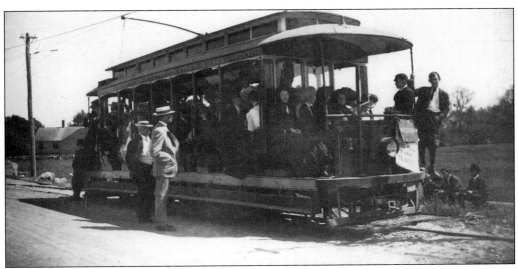

Here is a photograph of the Norfolk and Bristol Line, which ran from Mansfield to Foxboro. The line was often frequented by riders heading to Lakeview Park in Foxboro. A commonly asked question is why did the trolleys use so many side streets, such as through the Back Bay area or up Rumford Avenue? The answer is safety—to avoid a collision, the trolley cars were not allowed to cross the train tracks. One had to cross the railroad tracks by foot to catch another trolley.

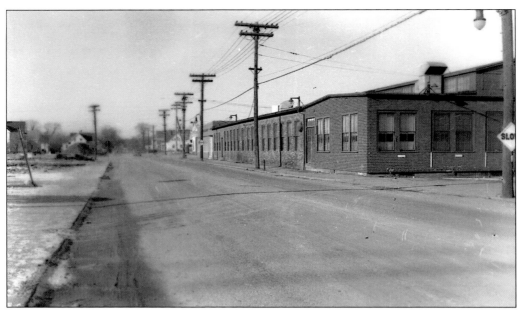

It is not hyperbole to say that the construction project that most changed the face of Mansfield was the installation of the three underpasses in the 1950s. This photograph reminds us of that, as we look at the still-familiar landmark of the Bay State Tap and Die Company complex as it appeared on Chauncy Street before the underpass was built. The total project cost was about $4,000,000. (Courtesy of *The Mansfield News*.)

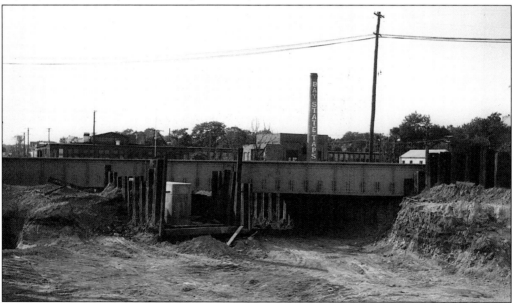

The Chauncy Street underpass sees the most traffic, as a part of busy Route 106. The project was begun in December 1954. During construction, traffic was rerouted over a temporary grade crossing behind Bay State Tap and Die Co. In addition, a quarter-mile stretch of the Rumford River was buried in a culvert, and Buck's Pond, located behind Card's Shop, was filled in for the project. (Courtesy of *The Mansfield News*.)

The North Common was once nearly twice its present size, as mentioned in chapter three. This photograph shows us how the common, at the left, was cut into for the underpass. The building at the center is the First National Bank. The old section of Chauncy Street that formerly gained access to North Main was renamed Thomas Street and is now an integral part of the one-way loop with North Main and Old Colony Road. (Courtesy of *The Mansfield News*.)

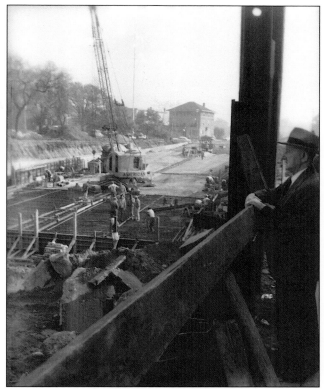

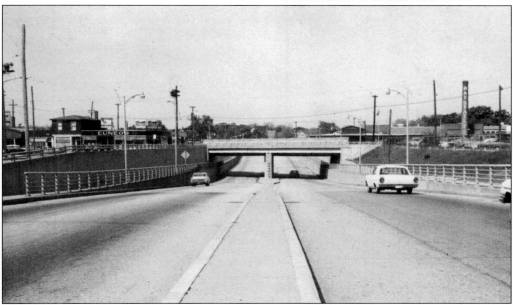

On June 7, 1957, the Chauncy Street underpass was opened to vehicular traffic, two and a half years after the groundbreaking. Several one-way and dead-end streets were created as a result of the underpass project. It also left stores like Cuneo's, seen here at the left, cut off from the main flow of customer traffic. The store formerly had a prime location in the old "Depot Square."

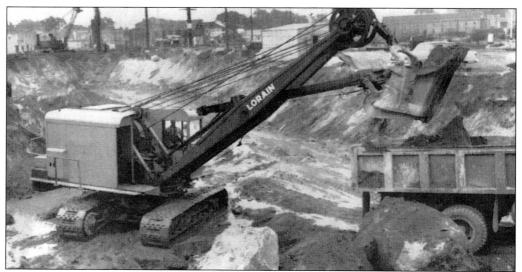

The North Main Street underpass also greatly changed the appearance of the North End. Here we see the construction looking south towards the downtown. The board of selectmen did not trust the new underpasses against flooding, and asked the railroad to leave open at least one old-fashioned grade crossing. Their request was not granted.

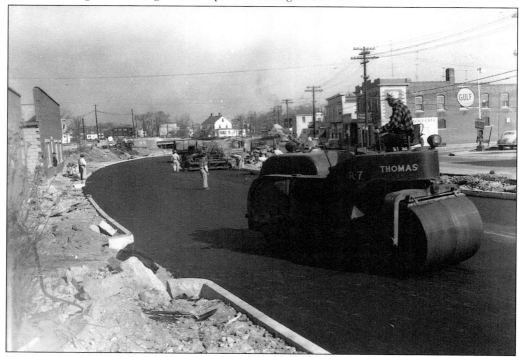

Paving crews are seen here entering the final phase of construction of the North Main Street underpass in November 1956. This photograph looks north, at the corner of Pratt Street. Jack's Cafe, which is now known as Geno's, is on the right. Another one-way loop of Oakland Street and Mansfield Avenue, connecting with Crocker Street, was created by this project. (Courtesy of *The Mansfield News*.)

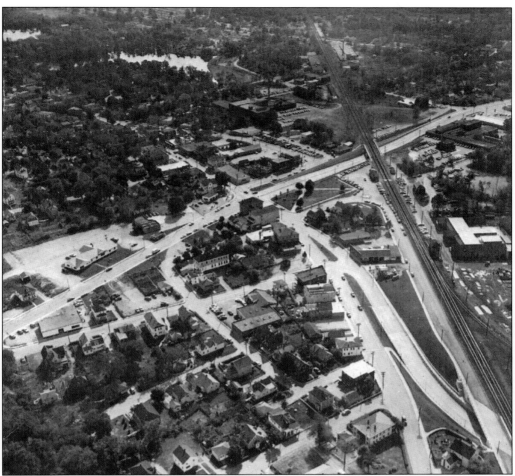

This impressive photograph graced the cover of the 1959 town report. It shows the downtown after the underpass construction. The layout is essentially the same today. In the lower right is the North Main Street underpass, and farther down the rail line is the Chauncy Street underpass. A close inspection of the picture shows many buildings still known today, and others that are gone.

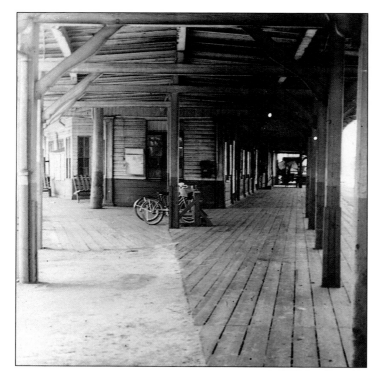

The massive projects of the 1950s brought progress, but left behind many memories never to be known to later generations. This almost ghostly image shows the station platform of the old depot as it appeared in 1938. The depot was demolished 14 years later.

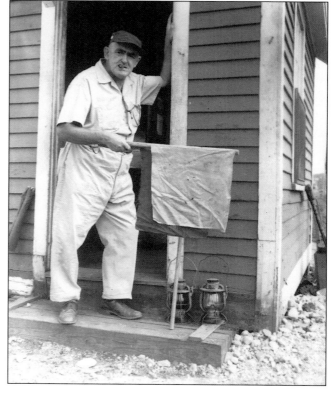

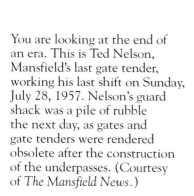

You are looking at the end of an era. This is Ted Nelson, Mansfield's last gate tender, working his last shift on Sunday, July 28, 1957. Nelson's guard shack was a pile of rubble the next day, as gates and gate tenders were rendered obsolete after the construction of the underpasses. (Courtesy of *The Mansfield News*.)

Five

ABOUT TOWN

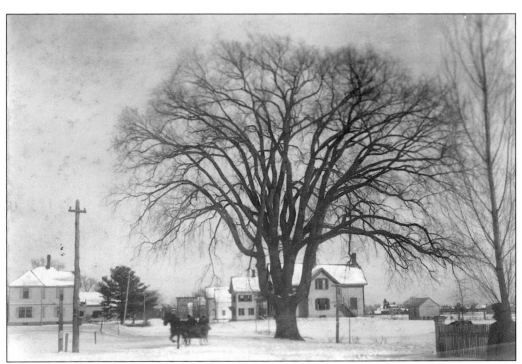

A stately tree graces this undated winter scene on Chauncy Street as we begin our look about town. This area, near the intersection of Chauncy and Central Streets, was known as Paine's Corner. The travelers in the horse-drawn sled are journeying away from downtown Mansfield. The large industrial building far down the road is the Rumsey Brothers Shoe Shop near Winthrop Street, which we will see later. We will now see what else we can find around town!

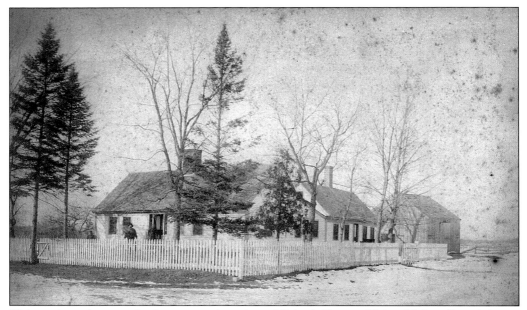

This ancient photograph gives us another view of Paine's Corner. This is Nelson Paine's house as it appeared in 1875, located on the northwest corner of Chauncy and Central Streets. One could only imagine what Mr. Paine would say if he could see today's heavy traffic in front of his quiet homestead!

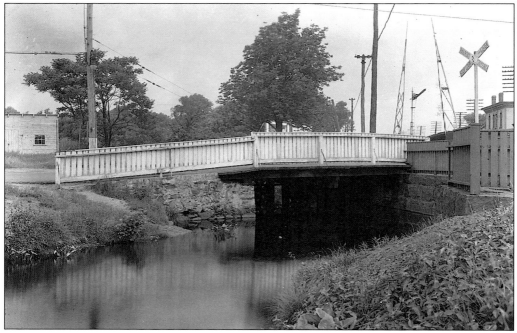

This wooden bridge over the Rumford River at Chauncy Street was once a main entrance into downtown Mansfield. A concrete bridge was constructed in its place in 1933, and the underpass replaced that in the 1950s. The Rumford River was also rerouted at that time.

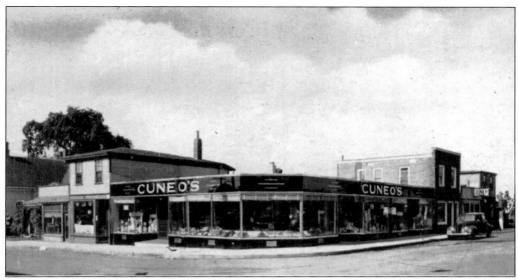

Cuneo's was a popular store that sold everything from tobacco and newspapers to beer and wine. It was in the heart of Depot Square, where Chauncy Street and Rumford Avenue once met. The building remains at the confluence of Rumford Avenue, Thomas Street, and Old Colony Road.

In 1858, Samuel B. Schenck constructed this famous building where Chauncy Street met the Old Colony Railroad. It had several names and many owners, but was best known as the Mansfield House. It operated as a hotel, restaurant, and watering hole for nearly 130 years. In 1933, owner Joe Roman obtained Mansfield's first post-prohibition license to serve liquor at the property, adding to the building's storied history. The Mansfield House was torn down in 1985. (Courtesy of the Mansfield Public Library.)

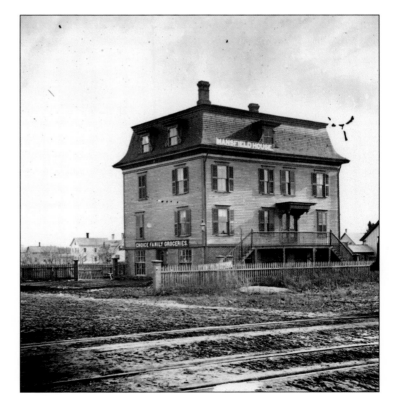

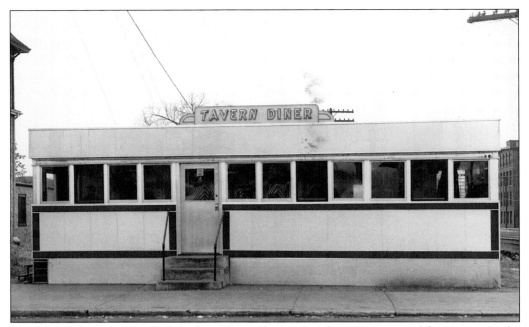

The Tavern Diner, also called the busy Depot Square area home, was owned for many years by Jim Clinton and faced Chauncy Street. The Mansfield House was to its left, and the corner of that building is visible in this c. 1949 photograph. The building remained in this location until it was moved to the new extension of Chauncy Street after the grade crossing abolition project. The building has since been demolished.

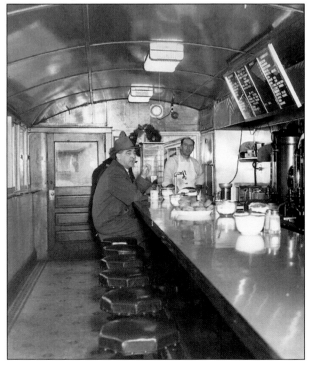

New owner George Pomfret is behind the counter of the Tavern Diner as a customer enjoys a meal. The diner featured typical diner fare, like baked sausage, meatloaf, liver and onions, and a roast-turkey special every Thursday. An immigrant from England, Mr. Pomfret started other successful Mansfield businesses, namely the Pomfret Laundry and later the Old Colony Diner.

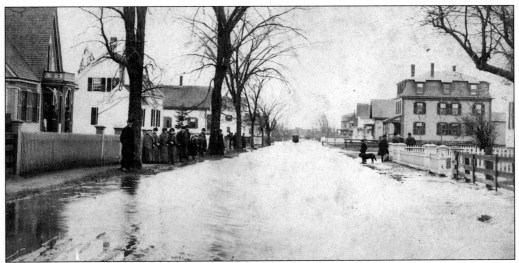

Never was a street so aptly named as Water Street after the Great Flood of 1886, a natural disaster that wreaked havoc throughout Massachusetts. This photograph was taken on February 15 of that year, before the name of the road was changed to Rumford Avenue.

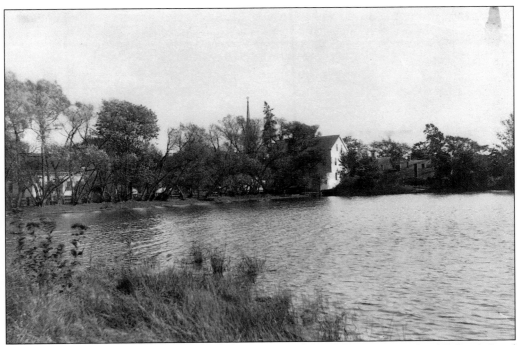

Thankfully, the height of the water was back to normal when this photograph of Fulton's Pond was taken in 1907. The building seen here was the Fulton Knife works, located on the shore of the pond. The steeple above the trees is the Orthodox Congregational Church on West Street.

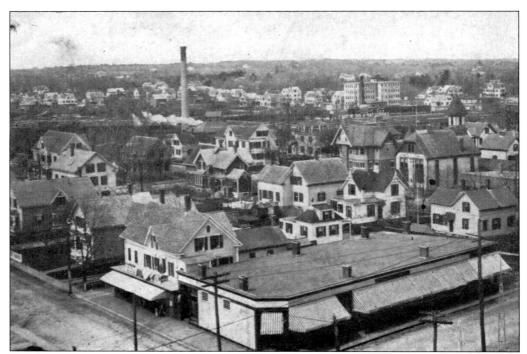

North Main and High Streets meet in the foreground of this shot of the downtown area. The building on the corner remains, but gone is Fox's store directly behind it. Other visible landmarks now gone are the fire station on West Church Street, the tall smokestack at Card's Shop, and the Rumsey Shoe Shop at Chauncy and Winthrop Streets.

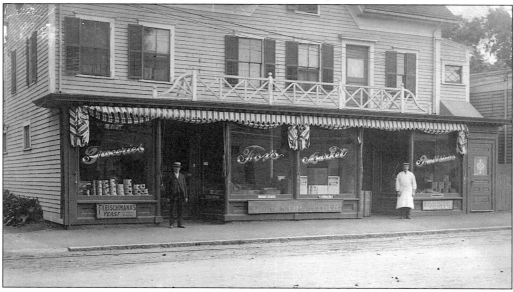

Here is a ground level view of Fox's Market at 7 High Street, another building known only by memory and photographs. This photograph was taken around the 1910s. The proprietor was Daniel H. Fox, and his establishment should not be confused with the nearby Fox Block on Main Street.

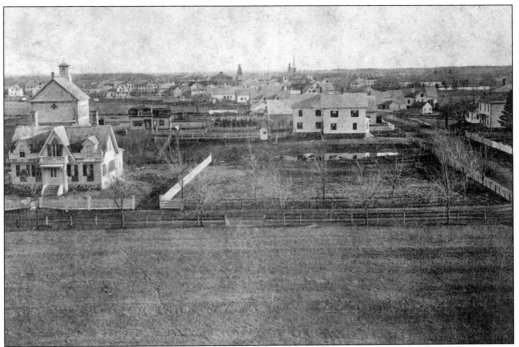

This early 1870s view of the Back Bay section of town was probably taken from the home of Gardner Chilson. The house in the foreground is on Pleasant Street, and North Main Street can be seen on the right. The rear of the original Saint Mary's Church on Church Street is visible, as the neighborhood appears to be more densely settled farther south.

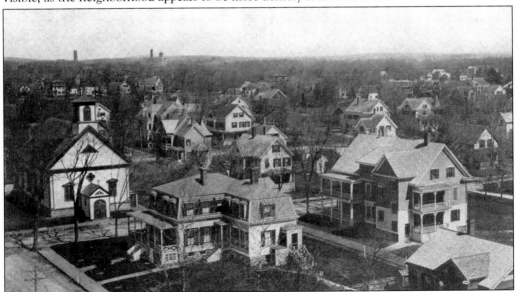

Another view of residential Back Bay reveals the intersection of Church and Bristol Streets at the extreme left, as well as the front of the original Saint Mary's Church. Across the street was the rectory, which still stands as a private house. Unlike our previous photograph, this shot looks to the north. It was probably taken from atop the grain mill.

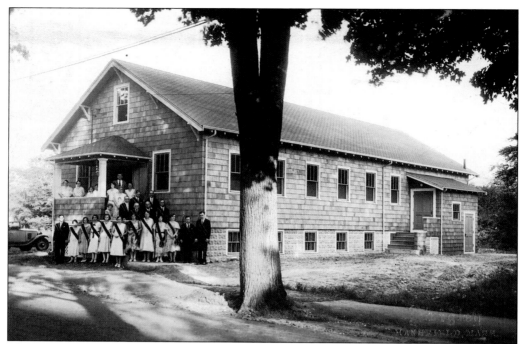

The Grange Hall on Park Street was headquarters for that organization for many years. In addition to serving the Grange, the hall was often rented for various occasions. The building, seen here in 1930, still stands at 13 Park Street. (Courtesy of the Mansfield Public Library.)

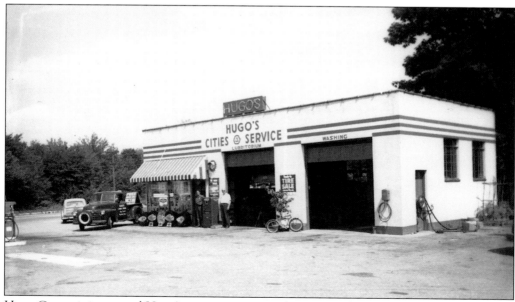

Hugo Copparini operated Hugo's service station at the corner of Hope and Pratt Streets. In an ideal location on a busy road, the station has changed hands a few times but is still in business as a gas station. (Courtesy of *The Mansfield News*.)

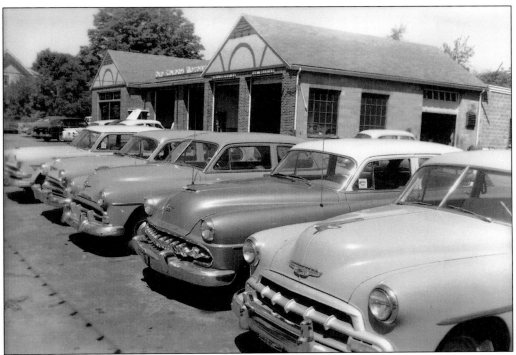

An impressive lineup of 1950s chrome and steel enhances our view of Old Colony Motors, another venerable Mansfield business. Founded in 1946, the Dodge dealership has expanded and now occupies buildings on both sides of West Street. (Courtesy of *The Mansfield News*.)

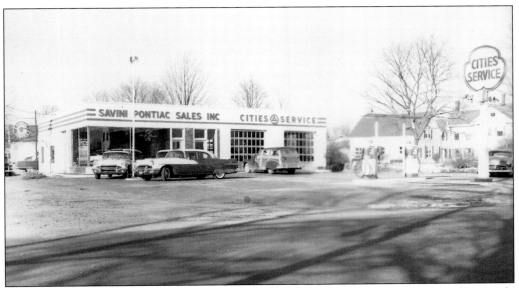

Savini Pontiac Sales, Inc. operated under several different names over the years. Previously Perry Motors, the name was changed after the business was sold in 1955. Situated at the corner of South Main and Horace Streets, the building now houses Allied Auto Parts at 95 South Main. (Courtesy of *The Mansfield News*.)

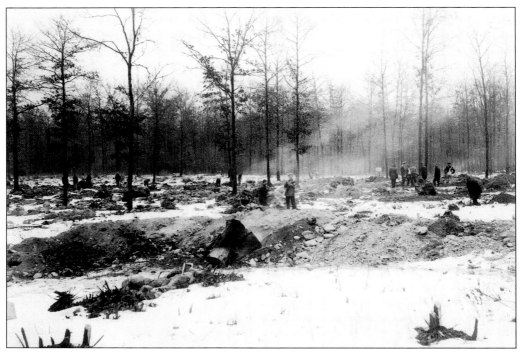

This may appear to be an unpleasant place to spend your free time, but when these workers completed construction in 1934 another Mansfield landmark was born. Memorial Park was built by the town in cooperation with the Federal Relief Administration in an effort to get unemployed folks back to work during the Great Depression. It has been a recreational center ever since.

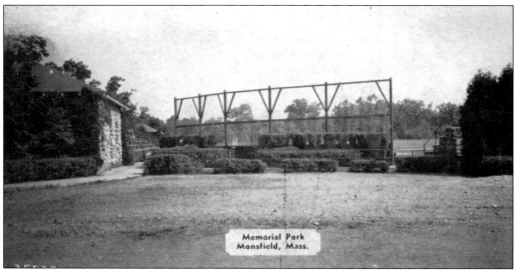

Memorial Park has long been an important spot in the Mansfield sports scene. The Hope Street tract of land has hosted Mansfield High football games for generations, as well as baseball games, softball games, and countless other types of sporting events. The tennis courts have also attracted many players over the years.

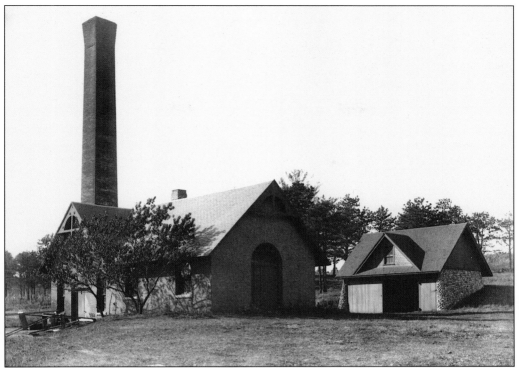

Mansfield's first municipal well was located here, at Cate Springs off Maple Street. The well was dug when Mansfield's municipal water system was installed in 1888. For decades Mansfield's water supply was hailed for its purity and good taste. Visitors were known to take bottles home with them, and natives enjoyed a glass whenever they returned from out of town.

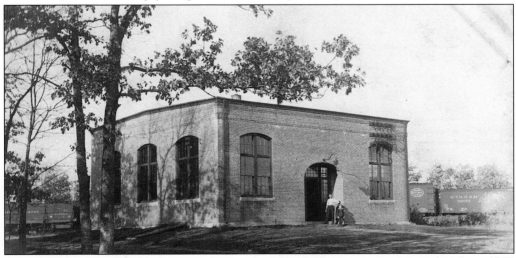

After two decades of feeble kerosene lamps, the Mansfield town meeting voted in June 1903 to build this municipal power station on West Church Street to light the roadways. Electric streetlights were installed and first used on the evening of February 23, 1904. The use of electricity for the home spread rapidly, and the light department has remained in operation since that time.

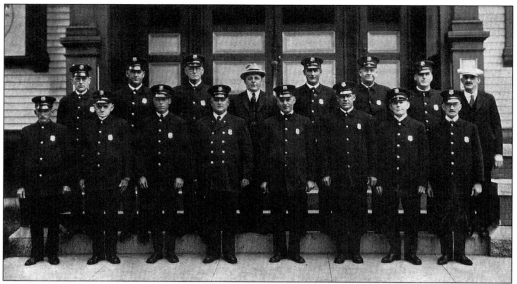

The Mansfield Police force posed for a photograph for the town's 150th Anniversary program in 1925. They are listed from left to right as follows: (front row) Pardon T. Leonard, Charles H. Kittrell, William J. Currivan, Charles R. Snyder, Arthur C. Conrad, Newell D. Vickery, James Newell, and Alphonso Buck; (back row) Ralph L. Williams, Rufus H. Ring, James E. Hannon, Town Manager William Plattner, John W. Conrod, George A. Ring, Carroll E. Phillips, and "Lockup Keeper" William H. Fuller.

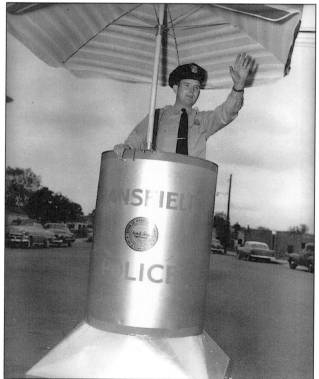

When the Chauncy Street extension opened in 1957, there was no traffic light at the intersection of North Main Street. Therefore, during the busiest hours, the police directed traffic through the intersection. Here we see Officer Edward Sliney directing motorists from a booth provided to the police by the Mansfield Lions Club. (Courtesy of *The Mansfield News*.)

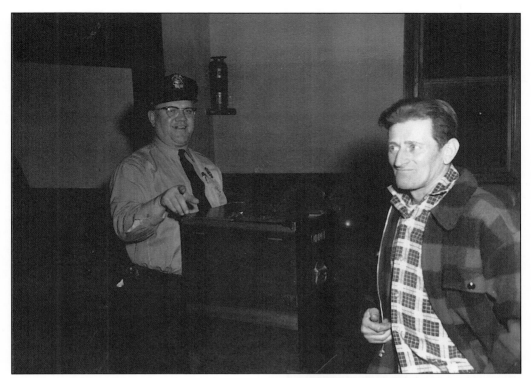

Patrolman Walter Johnson points and smiles to a photographer from *The Mansfield News* at the polls in January 1958. Johnson had just watched the last voter of the evening, Edward Epstein (right), cast his ballot. The '58 election saw Salvatore DeLutis elected to the board of selectmen, while Lewis Davison won a seat on the school committee. (Courtesy of *The Mansfield News*.)

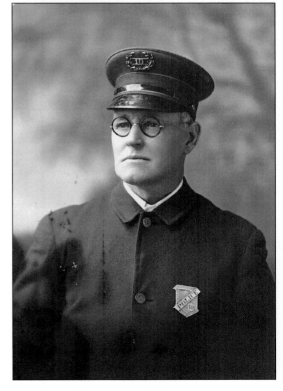

One of Mansfield's first police officers was James E. Hannon (1859–1934). A native of Westwood, Hannon came to Mansfield to work as a foreman at Shields's Foundry, a position he held all during his tenure on the police force. Also active in several local lodges, Hannon was called a man of "unfailing good humor." (Courtesy of the Mansfield Public Library.)

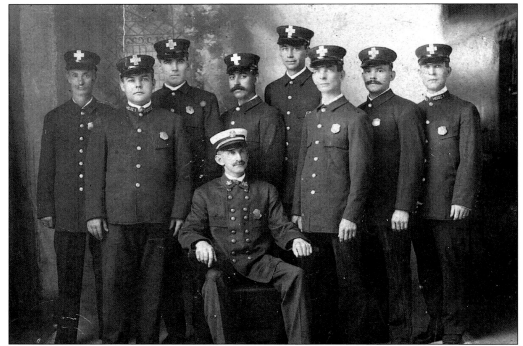

The Mansfield Fire Department also has a long history in town. Here is an early shot of the department. Pictured from left to right are the following: (front row) Chief Herbert E. King; (back row) Dave Higgins, Roy Martin, Dan Dacy, Arthur Valente, Arthur Soper, Wilfred Ball, Harry Fisher, and John Martin. It is interesting to note that in later decades, both Arthur Soper and Roy Martin would serve as chief.

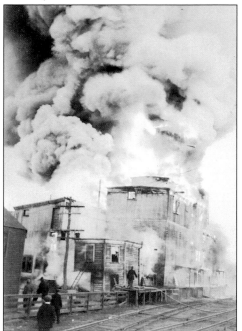

A devastating fire ravaged the Mansfield Milling Company on November 11, 1916. Located along the Old Colony rail line at Samoset Avenue, the building was commonly called the grain mill. The building was a total loss, and the fire so fierce that several nearby homes were badly damaged. The total damage was about $50,000, the most expensive blaze in town to that point. The company later rebuilt in the same location.

The Mansfield Fire Department called this barn on West Church Street home for 40 years. Constructed in 1890, the structure housed the majority of the town's firefighting equipment until the station on North Main Street was built. The old fire barn is no longer standing.

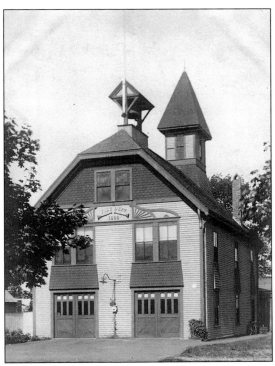

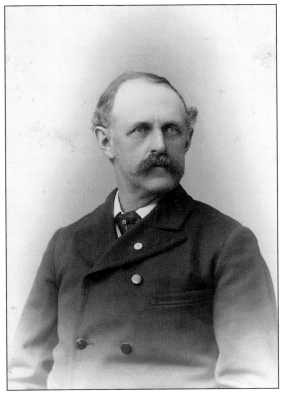

A most-respected man about town in the late 19th century was Alson Cobb (1841–1897). Cobb was in the Seventh Regiment of Massachusetts Volunteers as early as April of 1861, and fought in the Civil War for three years. Back in Mansfield, he was very active in several lodges and various other organizations, and was a deputy sheriff of Bristol County. He was also Mansfield's fire chief from 1891 until his death in 1897.

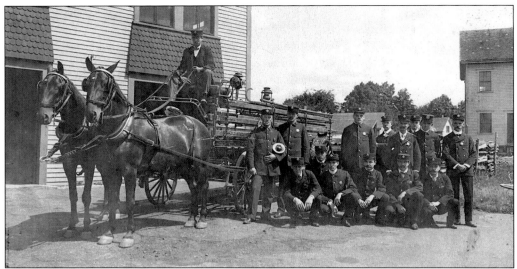

A horse-drawn fire wagon is an image that stands testament to how much things have changed over the past century. Here we see members of the Mansfield Fire Department posing in front of the fire barn on West Church Street, ready to fight a blaze with the best equipment available.

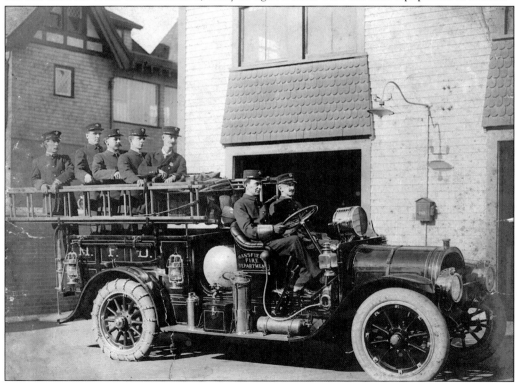

Times changed quickly for the fire department, as a motorized truck was soon their firefighting weapon of choice. Here are many of the same men from our previous picture. Behind the wheel is Arthur Soper, with Chief Herb King as his passenger. In back are Dave Higgins, Wilfred Ball, Arthur Valente, Dan Dacy, and John Martin.

74

Six

INDUSTRIAL MANSFIELD

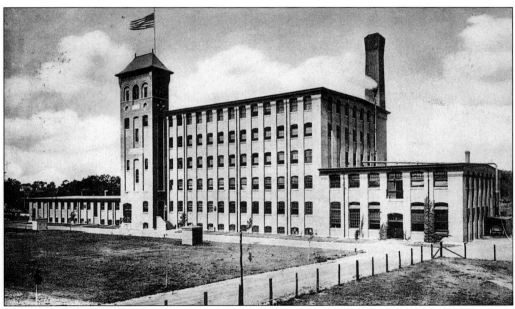

For a small town, Mansfield always had an impressive industrial base. Some factories sprung up in the center of town around the railroad, and a wide variety of products were manufactured here. By 1923, local industry had $4 million in invested capital, and a combined annual production of $7,400,000. We will start our tour of industrial Mansfield with what was probably the town's best-known plant, Lowney's chocolate factory on Oakland Street. Constructed in 1903, we see the factory as it appeared in 1907 before its massive addition was added on the left.

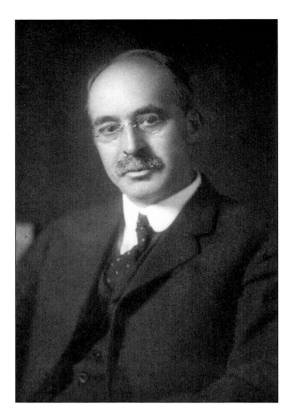

Walter M. Lowney (1855–1921) was born in Sebec, Maine, on September 2, 1855. From his humble beginnings, he eventually became a millionaire with his fortune built on chocolate. His first factory was in Boston, but he constructed his main plant in Mansfield in 1903. He took up permanent residence in town, and became the town's most prominent citizen and its greatest benefactor. He died while on a visit to Atlantic City and was widely mourned by his fellow townsmen. (Courtesy of the Mansfield Public Library.)

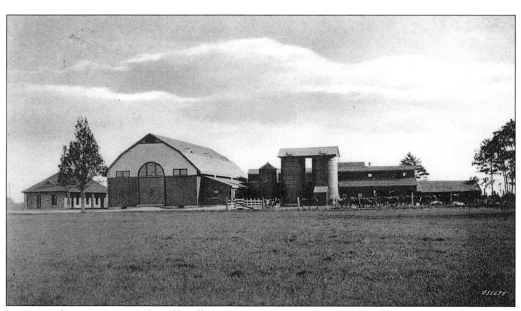

Lowney's factory was mostly self-sufficient. Here we see the Lowney farm, located off Oakland and Maple Streets, where thousands of gallons of cream were produced every year for the production of chocolate.

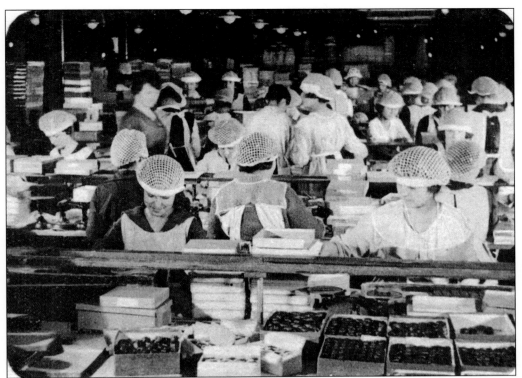

The packing room at Lowney's always hummed with activity. As this photograph indicates, the delicate work of handling and wrapping the finished products was generally left to women, providing them jobs in an industrial setting that may not have been available otherwise.

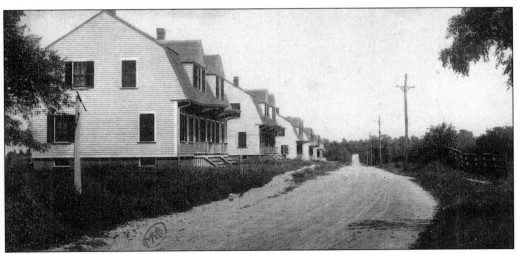

"The Lowney Houses" on North Main Street were built by the chocolate baron to provide affordable housing for some of his employees. In Lowney's time the houses were occupied mainly by Italians, the ethnic group Lowney is credited with attracting to Mansfield to build and work in his plant. Mr. Lowney was widely admired by his employees and in Mansfield at large.

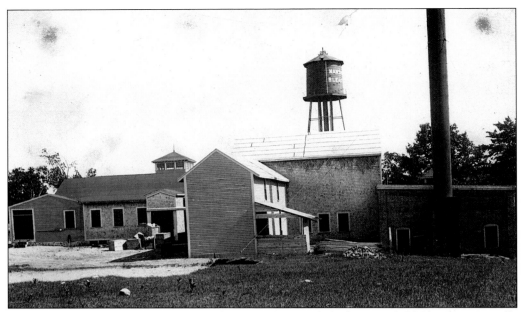

This is Mansfield's best-known landmark—in Foxboro! While the Mansfield Bleachery actually sat just over the town line of our northerly neighbor, the plant was always associated with Mansfield. The plant specialized in dyeing, finishing, and printing of fine cotton fabrics. It was nearby to other Mansfield factories and employed a great number of Mansfield workers.

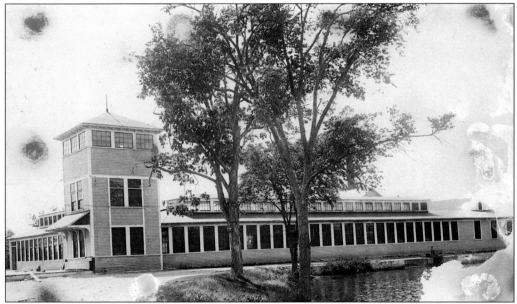

The Bannon family owned the bleachery and incorporated it in 1909, and then undertook massive expansion. By 1922, the complex had almost 2 acres of floor space for production, turning out 350,000 yards of cloth every week. The Bleachery Pond in the foreground was bisected by the road, and was a favorite swimming hole for generations.

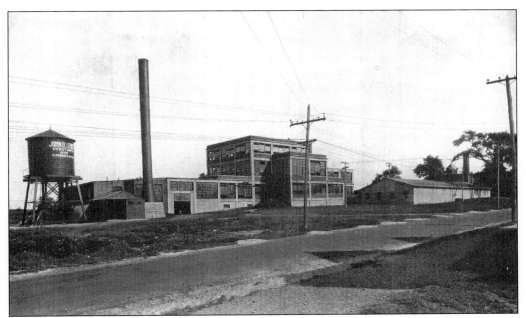

Originally a cracker factory, this plant on North Main Street has produced chemicals since the early 1900s. As of this 1925 photograph, it was known as the John D. Lewis Company. It was later known as Hercules Powder, then Blaine Chemical. The plant continues production today.

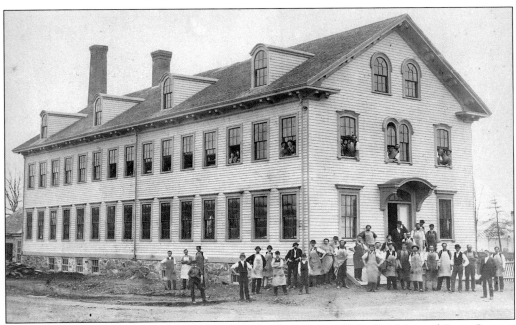

The jewelry shop of Doliver S. Spaulding sat on the corner of North Main and Pratt Streets. One of three such shops in Mansfield, the Spaulding firm produced jewelry made of pure gold, sterling silver, and tortoise shell. Production was at its peak in the 1890s, as Mansfield played a small role in the area's massive jewelry industry.

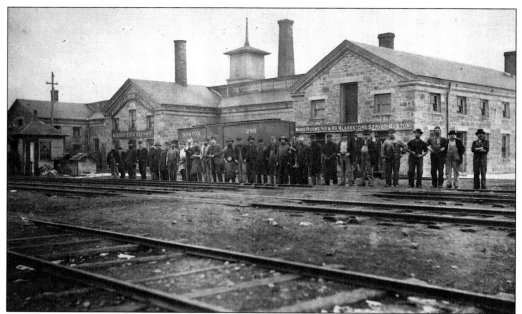

Gardner Chilson was a genius in the design of stoves and furnaces, and he built this plant to produce them in 1855. Located on the westerly side of the tracks across from the old depot, this photograph was probably taken around 1900. Chilson furnaces were used around the country and were widely hailed for their design, quality, and effectiveness. (Courtesy of the Mansfield Public Library.)

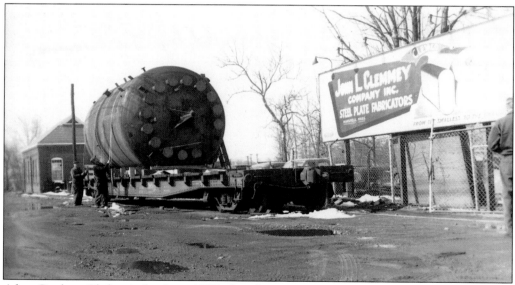

After Gardner Chilson's death in 1877, the plant continued production for some time. The building then had other uses over the next few decades, including a warehouse. In 1936, the plant became known as the John L. Clemmey Company, producer of tanks for various household and industrial uses. This 1956 photograph shows a food-processing tank fabricated by the Clemmey Company for a large food manufacturer. The tank was carefully transported on this railroad lowbed. (Courtesy of *The Mansfield News*.)

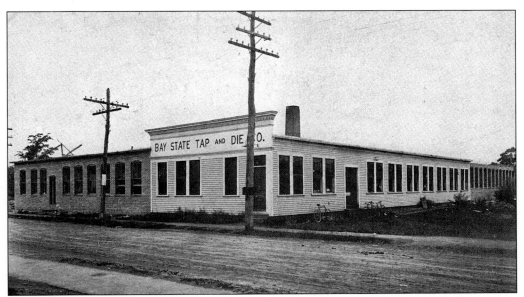

The Bay State Tap and Die Company was another industrial mainstay in Mansfield. Founded in 1903 by three Mansfield men, this photograph shows the Chauncy Street plant as it appeared in 1907, before it was the sprawling brick complex we know today. The factory produced taps, dies, screw plates, and twist drills until it closed in the late 1980s.

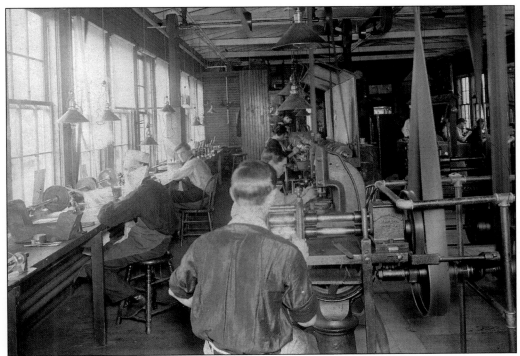

Walker and Davison produced gold pens here in Mansfield, another part of our diverse base of industrial products. Here we see the inside of the Walker and Davison shop, located near Bay State Tap and Die Co.

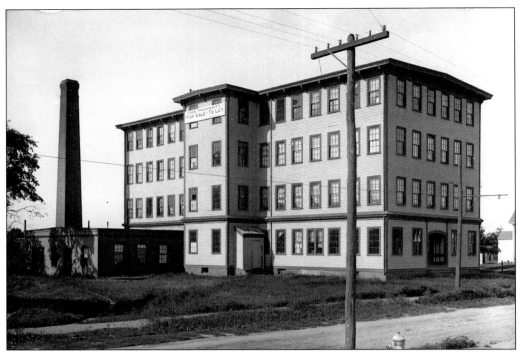

The Rumsey Brothers of Lynn established this shoe shop on the corner of Chauncy and Winthrop Streets in 1888, and remained in business there for ten years. The building next produced shoestrings, until it was bought by jewelry manufacturer C.D. Lyons in 1908. In 1919, the Bay State Tap and Die Company purchased it for storage, but by the Great Depression, poor economic conditions rendered the building useless and a wrecking company destroyed it at a cost of $500.

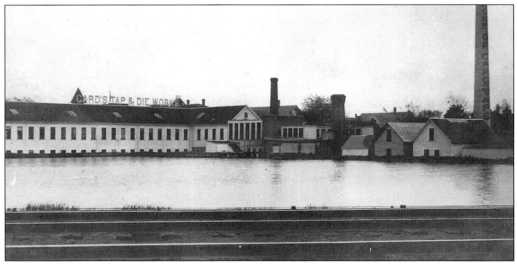

In 1874, Simon W. Card began his tap and die business in Mansfield. This photograph shows the greatly expanded operation around the turn of the century. The shop was located on Rumford Avenue, in front of Murphy's Pond (also called Buck's Pond) and the railroad. As we can see, the pond was created by a large earthen dam. The railroad tracks bisected the pond.

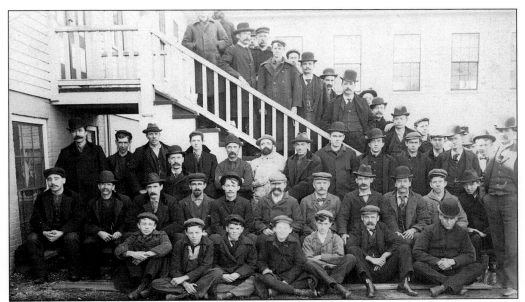

This rough and ready crew is an early group of workers at Card's Shop. As the business grew, hundreds would be employed at the plant, a good number of which lived in Mansfield. It has been said that his workers looked up to Mr. Card. They regarded him as honest and upright, and he was known to raise the workers' pay without being asked if he thought they deserved it.

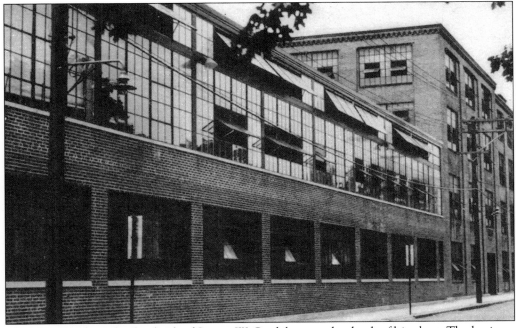

The year 1899 brought the death of Simon W. Card, but not the death of his plant. The business continued to grow, and in 1913 was bought by the Union Twist Drill Company of Athol, but was still known as Card's. The shop continued expanding through WW II, when it eventually became this familiar brick facade. The building is now the Millhaus condominium complex.

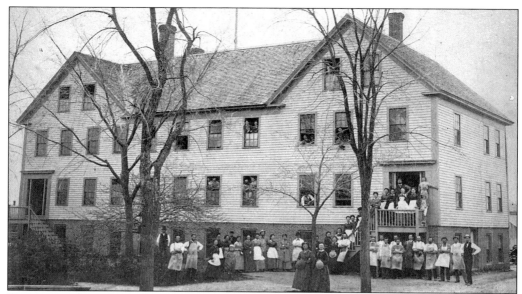

History says that John Rogers began to work with straw in 1835. Within a few successful decades, the firm of Rogers, Comey, and Company was formed and this shop was opened. Widely known as the Comey Straw Shop, it was located on Park Street along the Old Colony Railroad. The firm was bought out in 1919, and the new owners ceased operation after a fire in 1925.

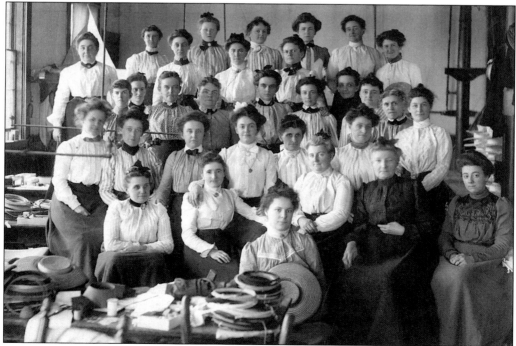

"The Straw Shop Girls" posed for this picture in the wiring room at Comey's. The "girls" could range in age from pre-teens to those over 80 years of age, but all enjoyed working together and often formed life-long friendships at the shop.

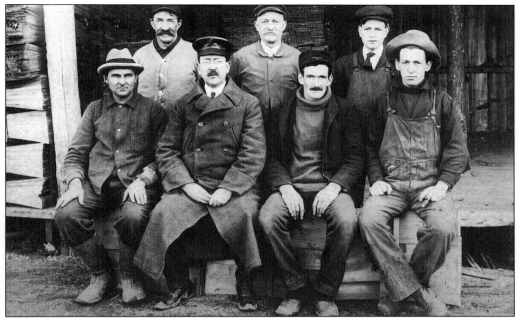

The Mansfield Lumber Company was located at the end of Webb Place, near the Old Colony rail line. The lumberyard consisted of several buildings in that area, most of which are gone today. This photograph shows several of the yard's early employees. Pictured from left to right are the following: (front row) Orrin Phillips, D.C. Richardson, William Berry, and Duke Gallup; (back are) Dexter Boyden, William Walker, and Stanley Tamblin.

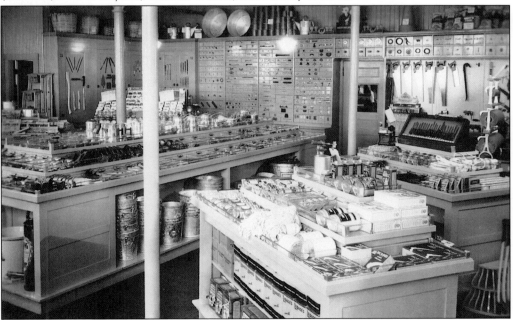

Established in 1895 by A.H. Richardson and J.A. Tuttle, the Mansfield Lumber Company was one of the biggest lumberyards in the area. In addition, the company maintained this hardware store for the convenience of its customers.

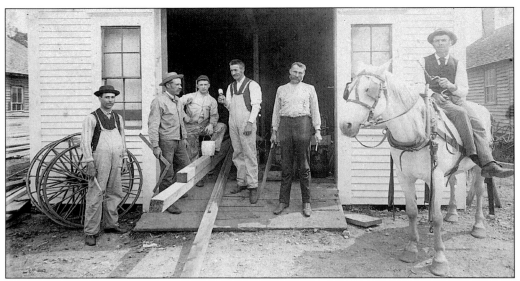

In the early 1880s, brothers Lewis and William Packard bought a piece of land at what is now 50 West Street. It included a blacksmith shop and a wheelwright shop. In this building, the Packards ran their sawmill. Lewis Packard, pictured here second from the left, was a longtime builder in town, constructing well-known structures like Masonic Hall, Wheeler's store (now 121 North Main Street), the former telephone building at 160 North Main, and countless houses.

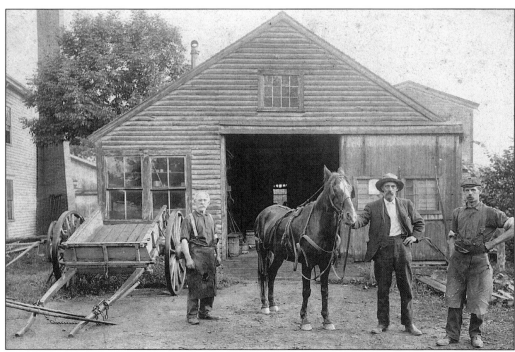

The Packards also ran a blacksmith shop on the West Street property. The first man on the left here is William Packard, Lewis's brother. William was a blacksmith by trade. The man on the right is identified only as Mr. Blake, blacksmith, but could be Frank Blake of Mansfield.

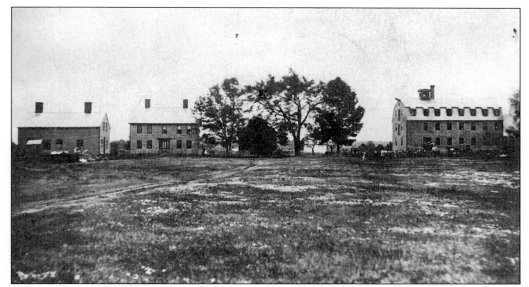

This 1871 view shows Union Street running through nothing more than an open field in the foreground. The buildings shown here are situated on Spring Street. The home whose front door faces the photographer is now a private residence at 56 Spring Street. The building at the far right is Cobb's shop, pictured below after remodeling.

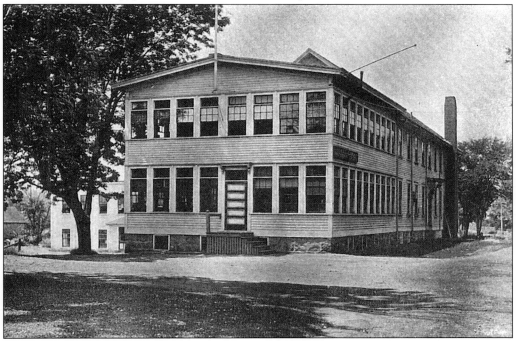

F.M. and J.L. Cobb's jewelry manufacturing shop was located on the southerly side of Spring Street, near the intersection with Union Street. The firm was originally called Cobb & Evans Company, until Frank Evans sold his interest to Frank M. and Justin L. Cobb. The shop has long since closed and other businesses have come and gone, but the building remains on Spring Street.

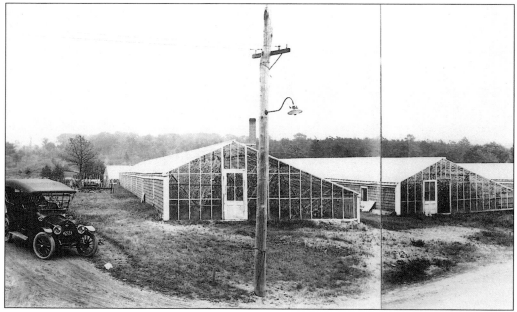

Benjamin Vickery started growing cucumbers in Mansfield in 1898, and in so doing, began a successful local industry. By the 1920s, 14 growers were producing about 20,000 cucumber bushels annually. The town had about 20 acres under glass for growing the vegetable. Here we see the cucumber greenhouses of George Geddes at 1246 East Street, c. 1910.

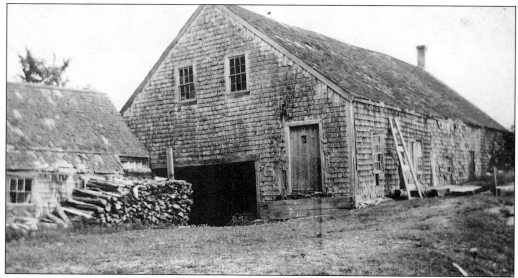

One of Mansfield's oldest industries was basket making, which was performed here at Fisher's Mill. The mill was located on Fisher's Pond off Willow Street. The basket-making industry began here when Abner Bailey took up the trade in 1793. The date reminds us that Mansfield has long had a fair share of industry.

Seven

SCHOOL DAYS

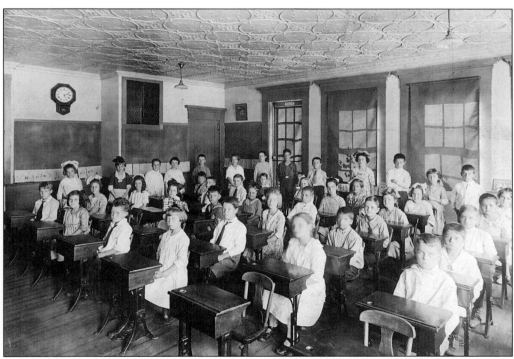

Mansfield has a long and proud history of supporting its school children. Here is a classroom at the Main Street School, probably from the 1890s. The school was also widely known as the Number Four School, from the time when Mansfield schools operated on the district system. Under that format, the town was divided into eight geographical districts, and the citizens of each district were responsible for the construction and maintenance of their schoolhouse. The district system remained in effect until 1882. We will begin our photographic look at Mansfield's schools by further examining the district schools.

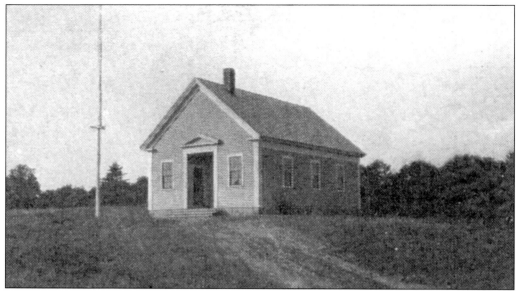

The Number One schoolhouse was in the village of Whiteville. The district had a schoolhouse as early as 1805 but this structure, located near the corner of Franklin and Winter Streets, was erected in 1854. The Whiteville School operated until May 1938 when the town sold it for $525 to the highest bidder. The remodeled structure still stands as a private home.

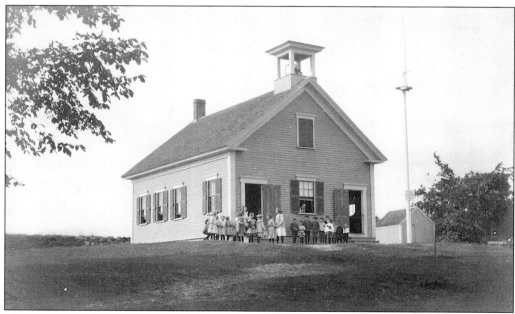

The Hartwell School served the remainder of East Mansfield. Originally known as the Number Two School, this building was constructed in 1881 when the previous Number Two School was destroyed by fire. Still standing at 71 Mill Street, the school was closed in February 1938. In the 1940s it was used as the East Mansfield Community Club, and is still owned by the town today.

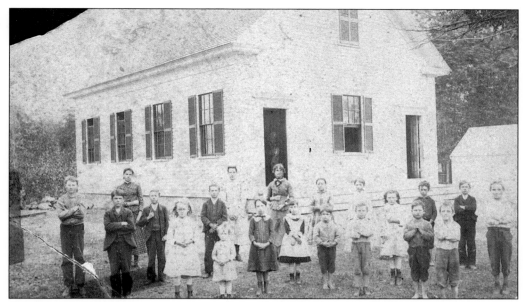

Shoeless school children pose in front of the Hall School in Mansfield's District Three. This structure replaced an older one in 1880, and remained in the town's hands until the selectmen sold it in 1943. The Fruit Street building was later used as headquarters of the Mansfield American Legion Post 198, until March 1995 when it was demolished to make way for two new homes.

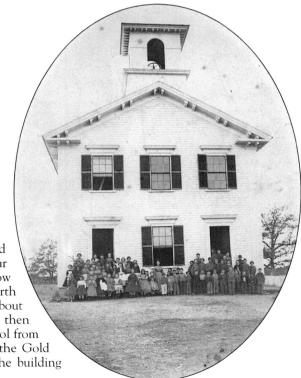

Here we see teacher Jennie Fisher and her class in front of the Number Four School, or Main Street School. Now the public parking lot next to 102 North Main Street, the school was built about 1854. Discontinued in 1900, it was then used as a boy's club. Revived as a school from 1918 to 1942, it was later leased to the Gold Star Amvets in 1950. Fire claimed the building November 21, 1959.

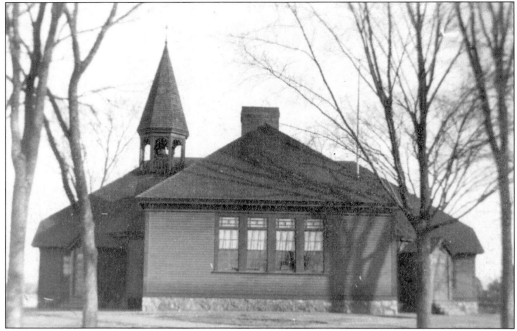

This photograph explains why School Street was so named. Located near the corner of School and Coral Streets on land now used by Spring Brook Cemetery, the Green School served District Five. The district had two school buildings claimed by fire until this one was constructed in 1887. The Green School remained until 1923, when fire struck a third time and the site was abandoned.

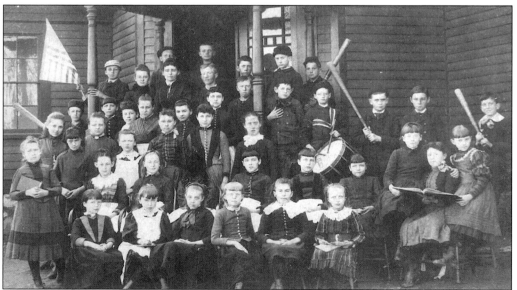

Green School students posed for this photograph in 1889. Newly reconstructed in 1887, the Green School was built at a cost of $3,700 by venerable Mansfield builder Lewis Packard. The three-room building, like many schoolhouses, had separate entrances for girls and boys.

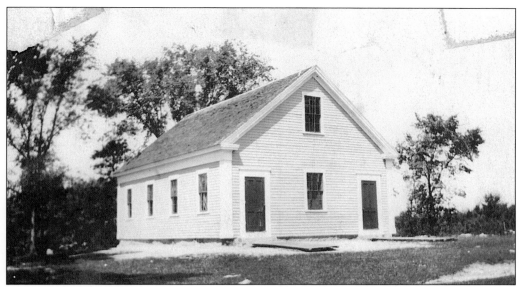

The Williams School, or the Number Six School, was one of three schools to serve West Mansfield. Located on Tremont Street, it was left an endowment fund by Rufus Williams, whose family was prominent in that section of town. As a result, the Williams School never wanted for money. Built in 1852, the school has been moved to 151 Tremont Street and is now a private residence.

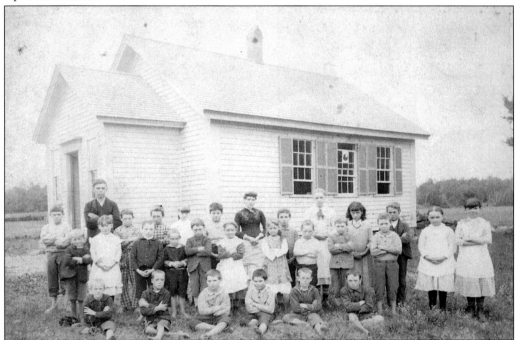

The Balcom School called the corner of Gilbert and Balcom Streets home. Located on what was once the main road from Worcester to New Bedford, local historians say the students were often distracted by the din of stagecoaches passing by the Number Seven School. A further distraction was the interesting activity at the nearby Balcom Tavern and Gilbert Tavern.

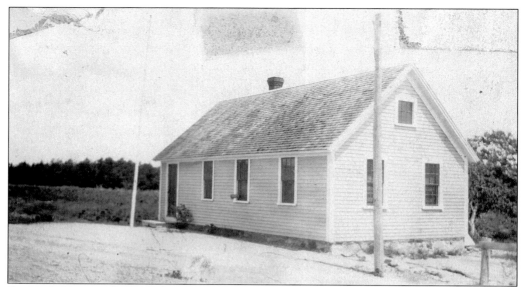

Pictured above is the humble Number Eight School, which was located on Elm Street. The Briggs School, as the building was later called, was poorly funded and usually lacking for money. Although no longer on Elm Street, the building remains in West Mansfield—it was moved to 44 Oak Street c. 1917.

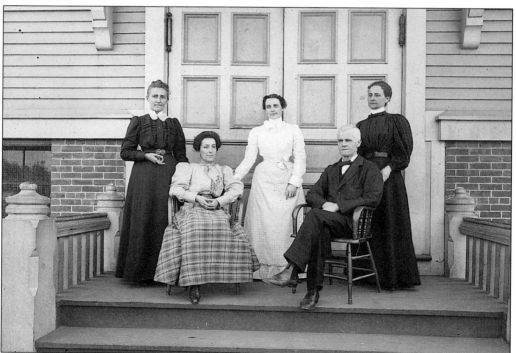

The gentleman seated in this June 7, 1899 photograph is John H. Berry, a most respected individual in Mansfield's educational history. Serving as a teacher and principal for many grade levels at several Mansfield schools, Mr. Berry poses here on the steps of the Central School with fellow teachers Lizzie Blake, Lucy George, Mamie Higgins, and Carrie Sheldon.

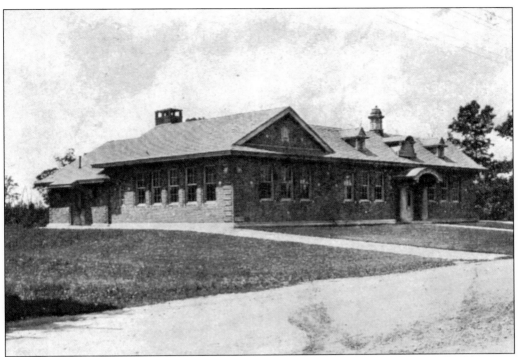

The John H. Berry School was built in 1915 in honor of Mr. Berry. This new building was designed to hold several classrooms, bringing about the closing of the Williams, Balcom, and Briggs Schools. The John Berry served the students of West Mansfield faithfully until its closure in 1981. The building was dormant for over 15 years, until the YMCA leased it in 1997.

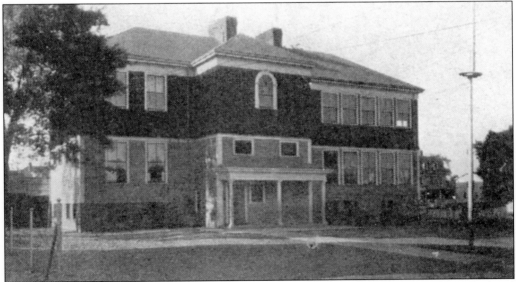

The Spaulding School lives on only in the memories of its former students. Located on the bend in the road at the southerly end of Crocker Street, the Spaulding remained in operation until 1981, when a school reshuffling led to three school closings. The building, then dilapidated, was used as a "Haunted House" by the Mansfield Jaycees, and was torn down in 1989.

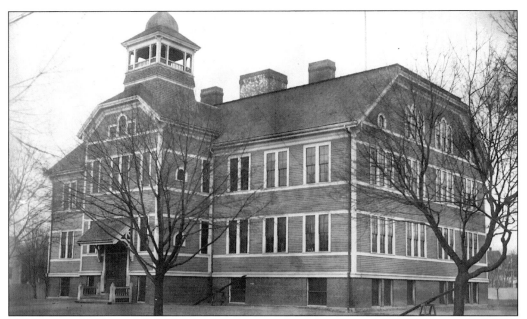

The spring of 1912 is the setting of this photograph of the Central School. Located on Villa Street, the Central School generally accommodated children between fifth and eighth grade, although it occasionally was home to others. The school is now gone, a commercial building standing in its former location.

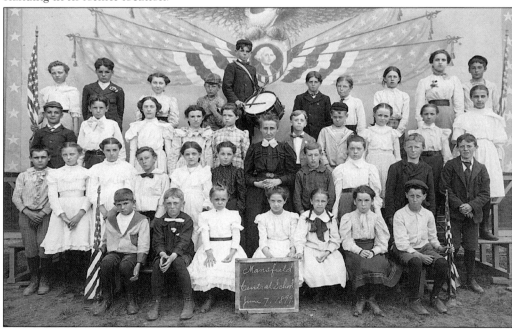

A patriotic backdrop is unfurled behind these Central School students, who posed for this photograph on June 7, 1899. The Central School never suffered a lack of students, as almost every Mansfield schoolchild attended the building in its heyday. An interesting observation in this photograph is that it was taken outdoors, as proven by the grass beneath the children's feet.

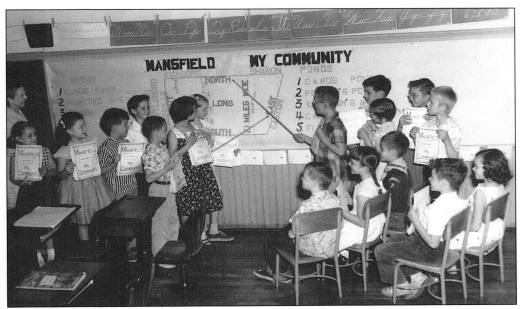

Miss Bellew's fifth grade class in the Central School studied Mansfield extensively in 1956. Here, the students explain the dimensions of the town, point out the neighboring communities, and highlight the town's rivers and ponds as they study "Mansfield, My Community." Courtesy of *The Mansfield News*.)

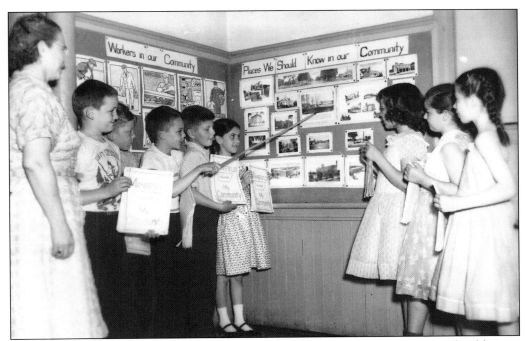

Here the students show Miss Bellew "Workers in our Community" and "Places We Should Know in our Community." It was Miss Bellew's hope that the project would inspire an interest in local history and a spirit of civic pride among the children. (Courtesy of *The Mansfield News*.)

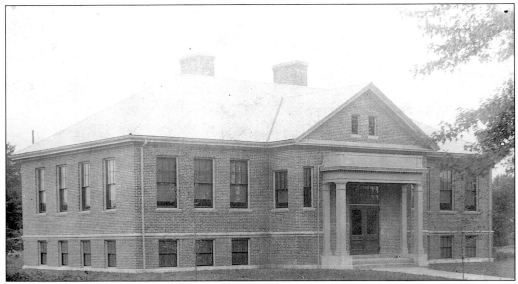

The Paine School generally housed elementary grades during its long service to Mansfield. Located at what is now the intersection of Chauncy Street and Copeland Drive, the Paine was the third and final school closed down in 1981. The town later used the building as municipal offices, until the new town hall was opened in 1997. The building has since been sold.

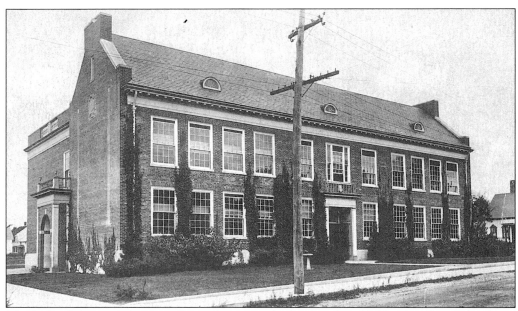

The Roland Green School on Dean Street was built after the old Number Five School was claimed by fire in 1923. Used by generations as an elementary school, the Roland Green has stood the test of time. The building is still used today by the school department.

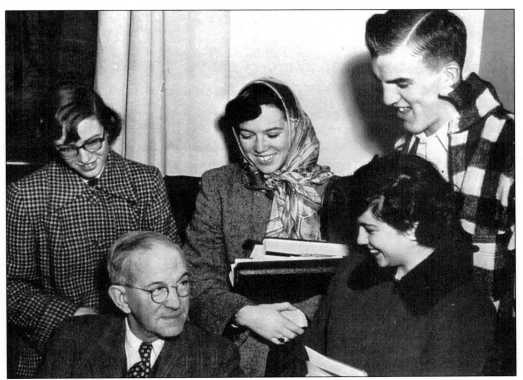

Everett W. Robinson, seen here talking to students in 1953, served the Mansfield school system in many capacities over his 38 years. Robinson was a high school history teacher, principal, guidance counselor, and even interim superintendent of schools. Active in civic life as well, Robinson served on the board of selectmen and as a state representative. The Everett W. Robinson School is named in his honor.

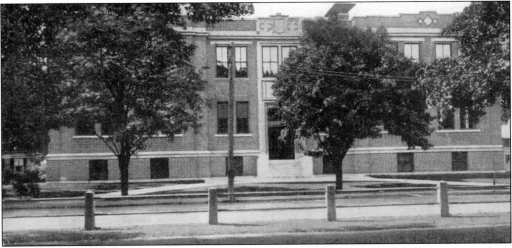

The Park Row School served many purposes over the years. Originally constructed as a high school in 1911, it served in that capacity until 1954. The Park Row was next used as an elementary school until 1992, and then was left dormant until it was revamped and opened as the new town hall in 1997.

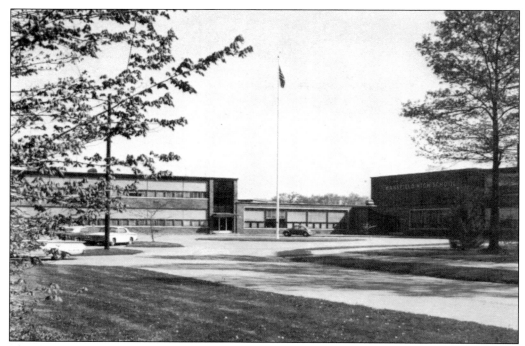

The new Mansfield High School on East Street was opened in 1954, and served in that capacity only a little more than a decade. By 1969, the current Mansfield High School was opened, leaving this building to handle sixth, seventh, and eighth grades. It is now widely known as the Harold L. Qualters Middle School.

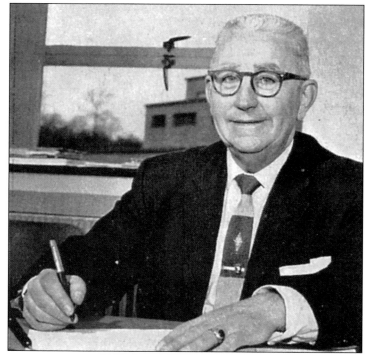

We close our section on schools with longtime school department employee Harold L. Qualters. Mr. Qualters taught at several grade levels over the years, and eventually became the principal of both the Central and Park Row Schools. In 1957, Qualters was appointed principal of Mansfield High, and in 1967 became assistant to the superintendent of schools until his death in 1971.

Eight

OUR CHURCHES

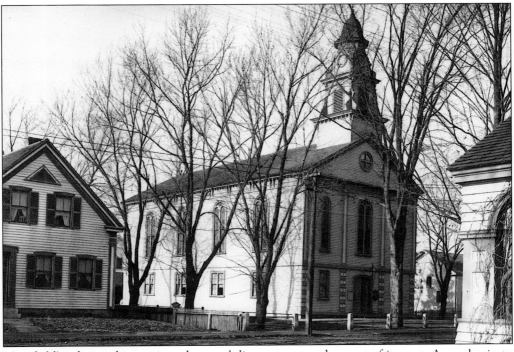

Mansfield's religious history is as deep and diverse as any other part of its past. As we begin to examine that past through photographs, our first stop is the First Baptist Church as it appeared *c.* 1900. Located at 52 North Main Street, this elegant church was constructed in 1838. A Main Street landmark for one and a half centuries, tragedy struck on the morning of April 10, 1987. A devastating fire gutted the building and left it a total loss. The remains were demolished, but the undaunted congregation rebuilt on the same site.

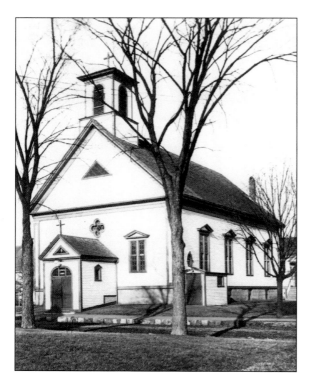

Saint Mary's Catholic Church was erected in 1871. Located on Church Street across from Bristol Street, it was served by mission priests until Saint Mary's Parish was formed in 1894. The building remained in use until it was claimed by fire early in the morning on July 29, 1914.

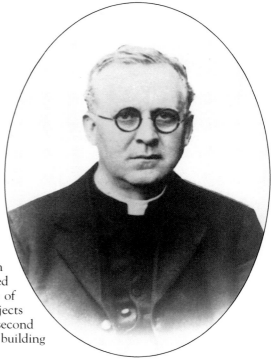

Fr. Hugh Harrold's 25 years in Mansfield was the longest term a pastor has served in the history of Saint Mary's. He served from 1910 until his death in 1935. An iron-fisted but beloved priest, Fr. Harrold was a native of Pawtucket who oversaw many important projects in his tenure, including construction of the second Saint Mary's Church after the original building burned in July 1914.

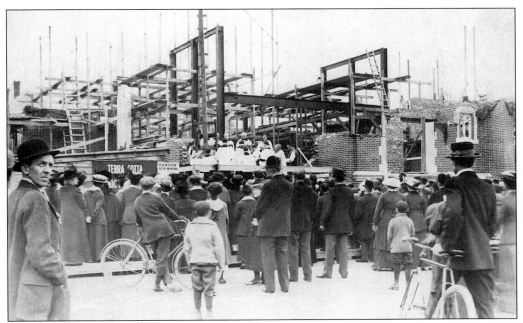

Bishop Daniel Feehan of the Catholic Diocese of Fall River came to Mansfield on April 19, 1915, to oversee the laying of the cornerstone for the new Saint Mary's Church. Here we see crowds gather to listen in at the historic ceremony, as the man on the left casts a curious and distrustful eye towards the camera.

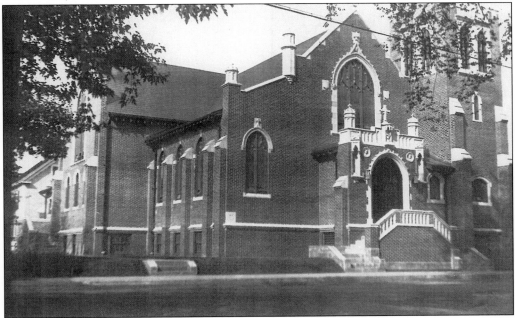

This stately church was dedicated by Saint Mary's in September of 1915, and served until the parish outgrew it in 1965. It was then used as a religious education center for two decades, and has sat idle since its closure in 1986. The church has since sold the building, and it remains on Church Street in a sad state of disrepair.

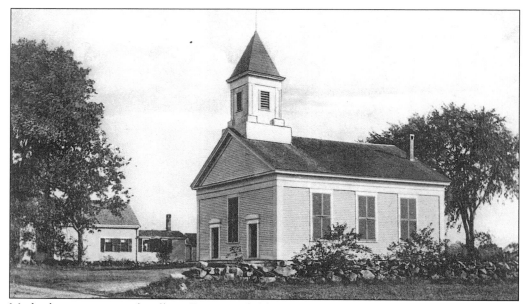

Methodism got its start locally in East Mansfield. The first Methodist meetinghouse in the area was built in 1810 on what is now the East Mansfield Common. In 1842, a sect broke away from that church over the issue of slavery and built this meetinghouse, still standing on East Street just beyond the East Mansfield Common. The building is now a private home.

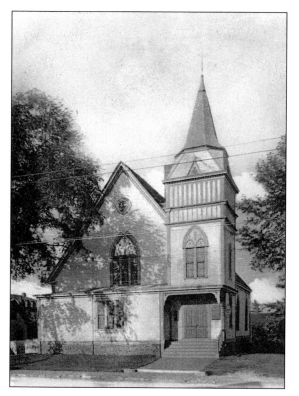

There was a small community of Methodists living in the center of Mansfield, and tired of having no house of worship, they organized, raised money, and erected this beautiful church in 1876. Standing on what is still the location of the Methodist church at 9 North Main Street, this structure originally had a towering steeple atop the belfry, by far the tallest in Mansfield.

Rev. Frank L. Brooks was one of the most active pastors of the Methodist church. An ambitious and brilliant man, Reverend Brooks saw that by 1913 the church had suffered considerable decay. He donated his vacation time and drew up plans for a new church. He then oversaw the stripping of the old one to its foundation, and the building of a new church in its place.

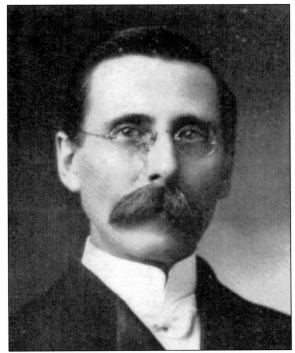

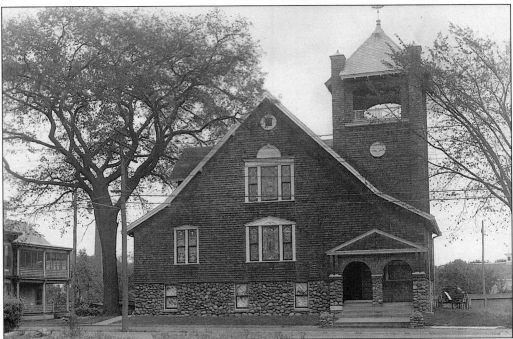

By 1915, Reverend Brooks's vision was complete. The Methodist society had erected this new church and braved an early spring blizzard to attend the dedication ceremony on Easter Sunday 1915. The Methodists still use the building today, which remains mostly unchanged over eight decades.

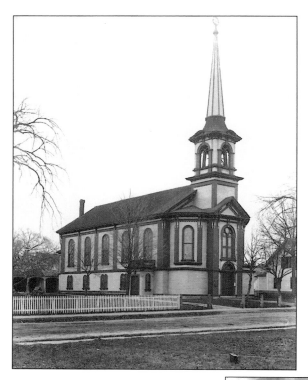

The Orthodox Congregational Church has a long history in Mansfield. The Congregationalists split with the First Parish in the 1830s over theological issues, and erected this church at 17 West Street at a cost of about $3,500. The church was greatly remodeled in 1871 and 1872, when it took on the appearance seen here and known to Mansfield residents today.

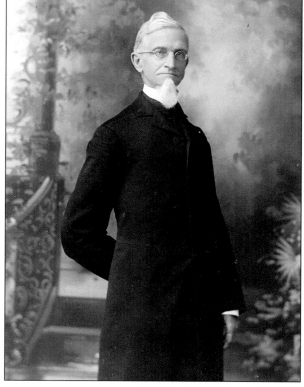

The Reverend Jacob Ide (1823–1898) preached at the Congregational church for 42 years, from 1856 until his death. A native of Medway, Reverend Ide was more than a beloved pastor to Mansfield as his civic spirit added much to the town. Reverend Ide served as state representative and state senator, and was instrumental in the push to open a public library in Mansfield. (Courtesy of the Mansfield Public Library.)

The First Christian Church of West Mansfield met in a small meetinghouse on Jewell Street from the 1830s until it outgrew the building. In 1873, this new church had been built on the corner of Elm and Otis Streets as the new place of worship. The society continued to meet in the building until one tragic day in 1919, when fire destroyed the dignified old structure.

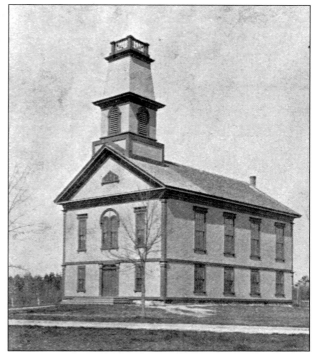

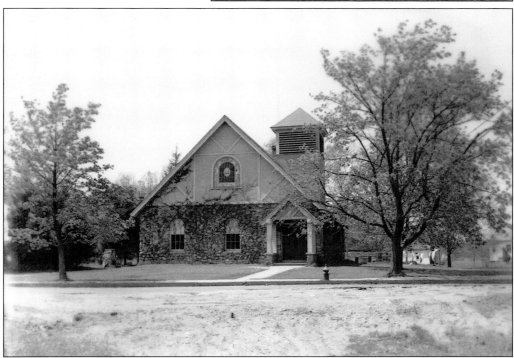

The congregation of the First Christian Church was undaunted by the fire, and rebuilt. This unique wood and stone edifice replaced the old building. The new church continues to be a familiar landmark to Mansfield residents, still standing at 11 Otis Street in West Mansfield.

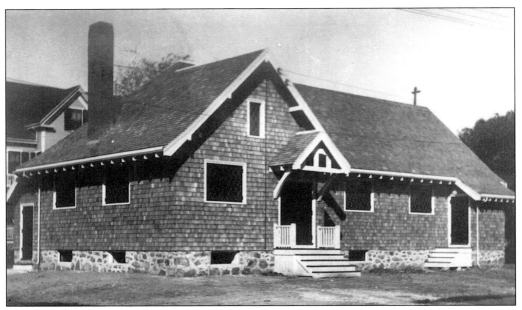

This view, taken in October of 1908, shows Saint John the Evangelist Episcopal Church as it appeared then. The building still stands at 47 High Street, on the corner of Rumford Avenue. Although additions have since been made and some remodeling has occurred, the building still looks essentially the same today. There is a bell from the works of Paul Revere in the belfry.

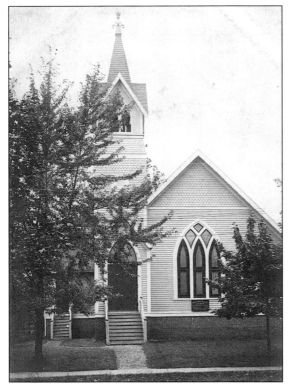

The First Universalist Church of Mansfield moved into these quarters on Rumford Avenue in 1888. The parish was formed out of the First Congregational Parish, which formerly met at the old meetinghouse. This church still stands on Rumford Avenue, now a private home.

The New Jerusalem Church, also known as the Swedenborgen Church, still stands as a private residence at 98 West Street. The Reverend George F. Stearns was pastor when this 1896 photograph was taken. The Swedenborgen Church remained until 1975, when the congregation dwindled and the building was sold.

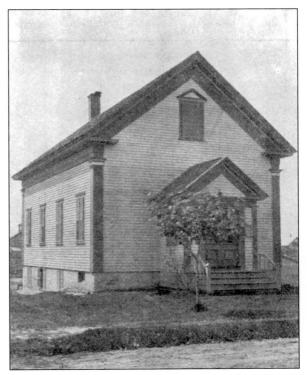

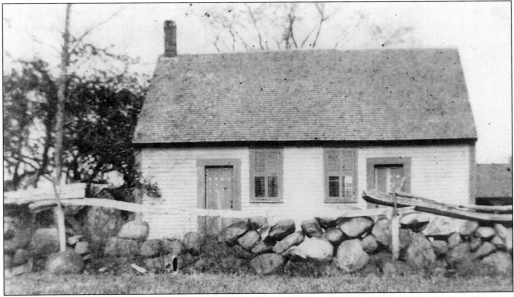

The humble Quaker meetinghouse, which stood on Williams Street, has a fascinating history. The Friends Society was organized around 1800, and the meetinghouse had separate doors and separate meetings for men and women. The society slowly died out in the early 20th century, and the last Mansfield Quaker died about 1920. The meetinghouse sat dormant for about ten years after that, until members of the Smithfield Society of Friends came to Mansfield and tore it down.

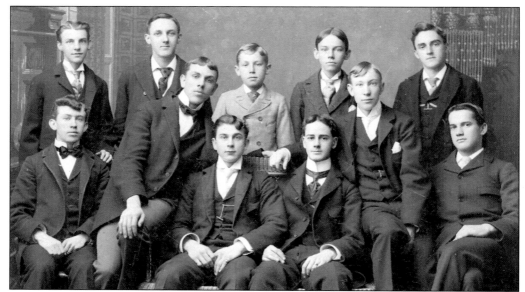

These dapper and upright young lads were a part of Mr. Fitts's Sunday school class at the Orthodox Congregational Church in 1892. In the front row are Frank Angell, Ernest Greene, Charlie Webb, Charles Hardon, George Hudson, and Howard Paine. In the back row are Charlie and Ozzie Corey, but the others are unknown.

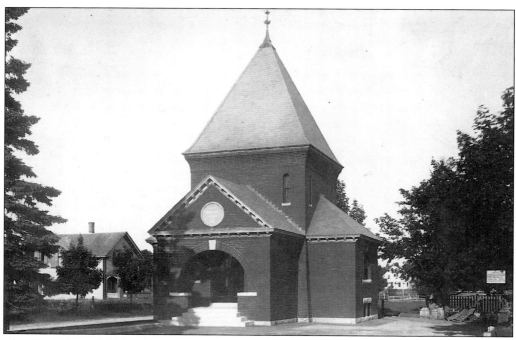

The Card Memorial Chapel was erected in 1898 by Mr. and Mrs. Simon W. Card in memory of their only child, Mary Lewis Card. Miss Card died in her early thirties, and had been extensively involved in her father's business. Located on Spring Street in Spring Brook Cemetery, the chapel was erected by the bereaved parents "for such public use as its character indicates."

Nine

EAST AND WEST MANSFIELD

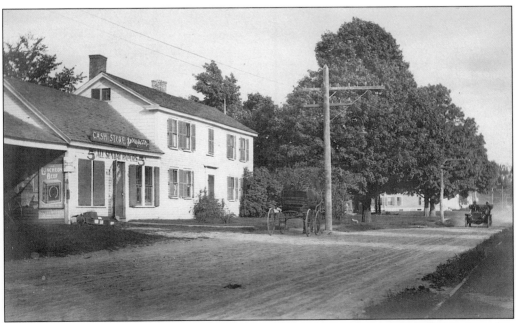

Both East and West Mansfield have had interesting and unique histories with distinctions that separate them from the rest of town. We will start our look at the outskirts with some scenes from East Mansfield. This cash store stood at 974 East Street, opposite the East Mansfield Common. The signs in front of the store advertise bread, pastry, and all Sunday newspapers for 5¢ in this photograph c. 1910s. At the time, the local stores were very important, as a trip into town was not an everyday occurrence.

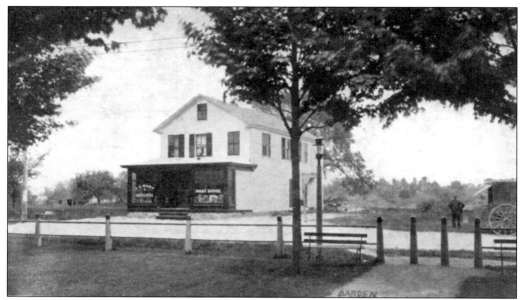

East Mansfield had not only its own post office, but also had its own zip code: 02031. The office is pictured here as it once appeared at 962 East Street facing the East Mansfield Common. The East Mansfield Post Office changed locations, but remained open until April 13, 1998, when the office was closed and all postal business was directed to the main post office downtown.

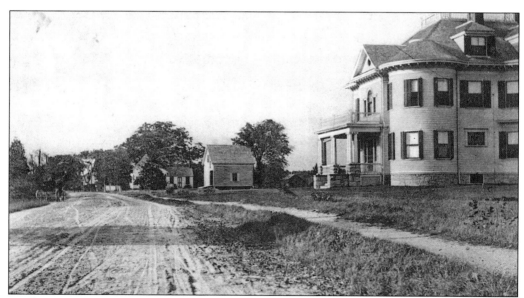

It is hard to imagine East Mansfield today without the hundreds of new houses that have arisen there over the past 30 years, but when this photograph of East Street was taken around the 1910s, this section was considered heavily populated. This photograph was taken between Flint's Farm and the East Mansfield Common, and the unique home on the right still stands at 912 East Street.

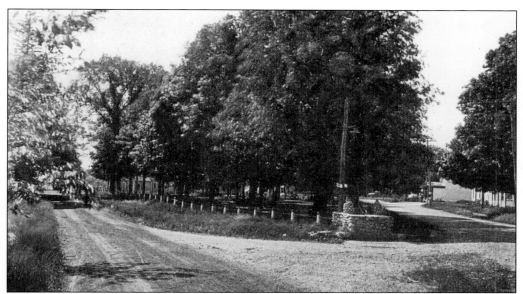

This is how the East Mansfield Common appeared when this photograph was taken in 1925. The road running to the left is Cherry Street, and at the right is East Street. Much like the South Common in the center of town, this common has changed in many respects over the years, while still retaining much that is recognizable today.

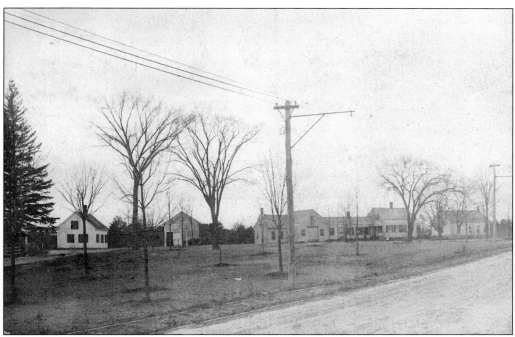

Here is a slightly earlier view of the East Mansfield Common, from East Street looking back towards Mill Street in 1907. Originally containing 1.5 acres of land, the common was once home to the First Methodist Church of East Mansfield. An interesting observation is the trolley tracks running down East Street, serving passengers from downtown Mansfield to Easton.

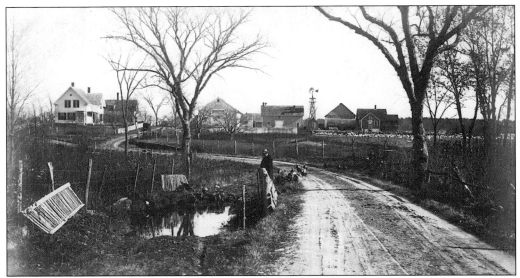

The Austin Goose Farm was in the Whiteville section of East Mansfield, located on the familiar bend in the road on Winter Street. A driveway separates the farmhouse from the barn. Begun in 1867, the Austin Goose Farm was reputed to be the largest poultry farm in the world, handling in one year, 25,000 geese; 12,000 ducks; 14,000 turkeys; and 100,000 hens and chickens.

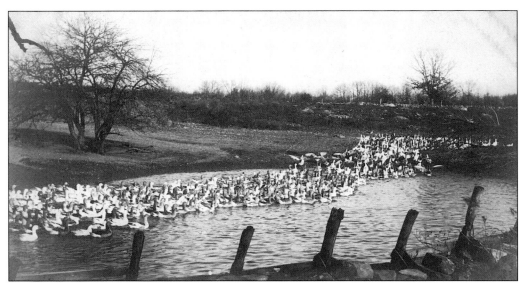

Here we see birds from the Austin Goose Farm go for a swim in Whiteville Pond, located next to the farm property. The Austins purchased their poultry mostly from Prince Edward Island, but also from Quebec, Rhode Island, and the western United States. Usually it arrived in Mansfield by train and was marched up to the farm in a large parade. A housing subdivision now stands where the Austin Goose Farm once was.

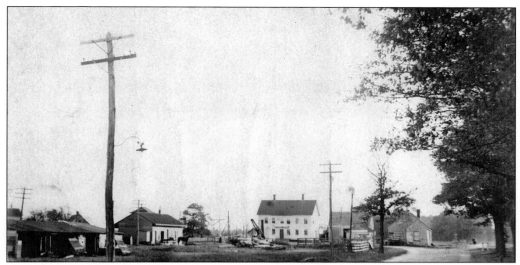

West Mansfield has always been a unique village in its own right. This West Mansfield scene shows much that we would still see today. At the left is the West Mansfield train station. The white building at the center is now the main entrance to the Old Country Store, and the road running down the right is Otis Street.

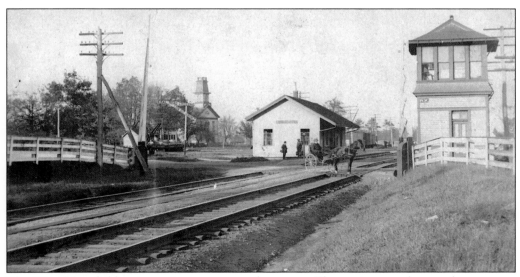

The West Mansfield train station was once a busy spot. The station stood near what we now know as the parking lot to the Old Country Store on Otis Street. At the right is a signal tower to assist with train traffic along the busy route. Visible in the distance at the left is the First Christian Church before it was claimed by fire in 1919.

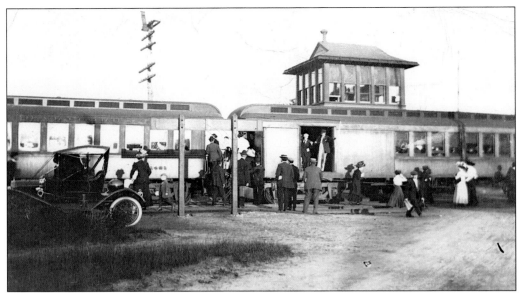

Here is another view of the West Mansfield train station, as it appeared *c.* 1910. Passengers are seen boarding and disembarking from the train, proof that the station was a regular stop on the Boston to Providence line just like the center of town.

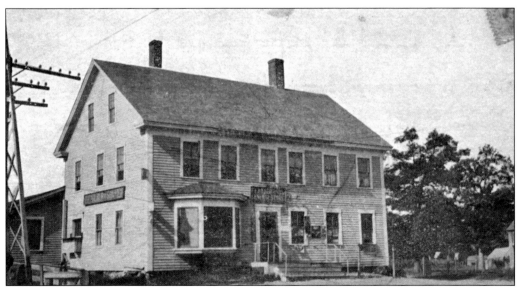

The Old Country Store has been in operation for many generations in West Mansfield. This early view of the store may seem unfamiliar at first, but much of the original store has been preserved. The store's old-fashioned quaintness that remains today makes it an attraction to shoppers for miles around.

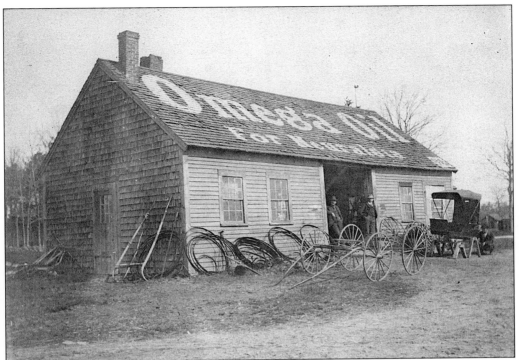

The blacksmith shop of Thomas Cutting, Frank Williams, and Louis Cutting was important to West Mansfieldians a few generations ago. Much like the general stores on the outskirts of town, this blacksmith shop was important because West Mansfield residents did not frequently travel downtown, causing village services to be a necessity.

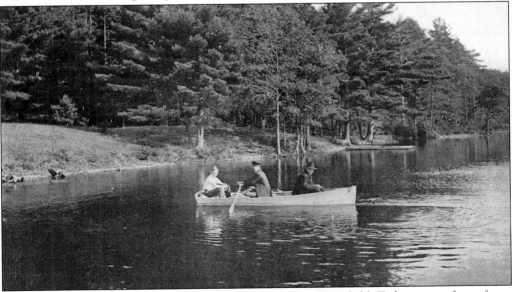

This bucolic view was taken on Greenwood Lake in West Mansfield. Today, most of us refer to the body of water as Bungay Lake, but no matter what the lake was called it has always been a source of enjoyment for the people in the area.

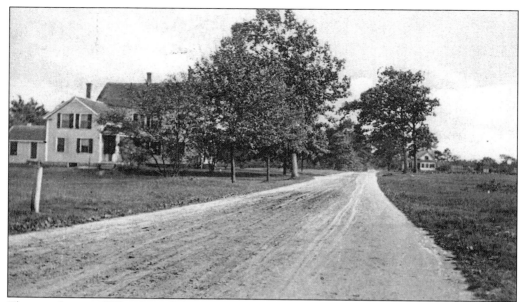

The population of West Mansfield has also soared over the past 30 years, leaving us to imagine the town as it must have looked during a more rural time. This meandering country road is Elm Street, now a much wider and more heavily traveled thoroughfare.

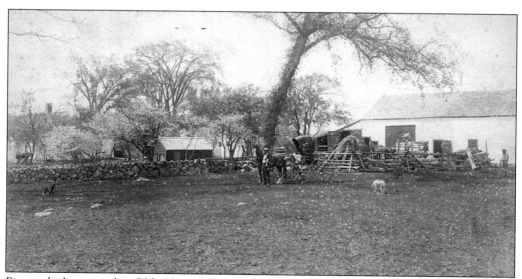

Pictured above is the Old Glory farm called West Mansfield home for many years. This photograph shows the property as it appeared in 1885. Today the land formerly occupied by the Old Glory farm is home to the Tri-County Beagle Club at 440 School Street.

Ten

PEOPLE, PLACES, AND FACES

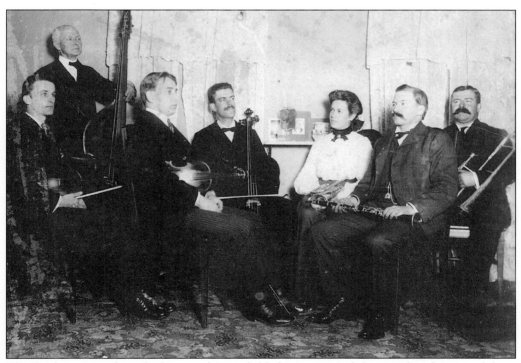

The final section of our look around Mansfield shows some of the people, places, and faces that made Mansfield unique over the years. Here we see a Mansfield band from the early 20th century. Standing in the rear is Elvin Smith on the bass viol. Seated from left to right are the following: Raymond Wheeler, violin; Arthur Appleby, violin; Will Lovell, cello; Grace Holden Williams, cornet; George Clapp, cornet; and Walter Huston, trombone.

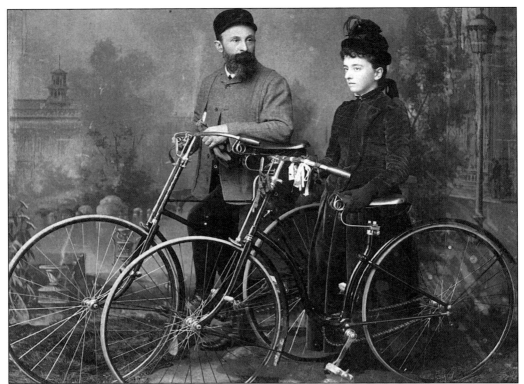

Horace Dryden and his daughter Linnie posed for J. Ralph Allen in this portrait. The following 1890 quote from *The Mansfield News*, discovered by Jennie Copeland, indicates that Linnie was at the forefront of female bicycle riding in Mansfield: "Linnie Dryden, a Mansfield pioneer lady bicyclist, is riding her new Vulcan light roadster . . . very gracefully."

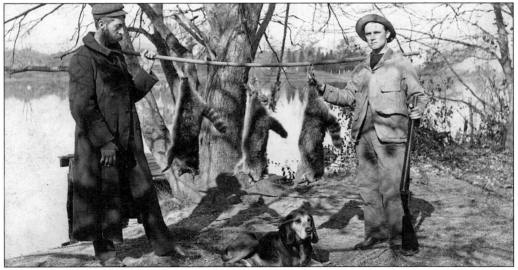

Life on the frontier? No, it's just Charles Gallup and Albert T. Hodges on a "Coon Hunt" right here in Mansfield, c. 1898. Judging by the photograph, it appears the hunters and their dog had a much better day than the raccoons did!

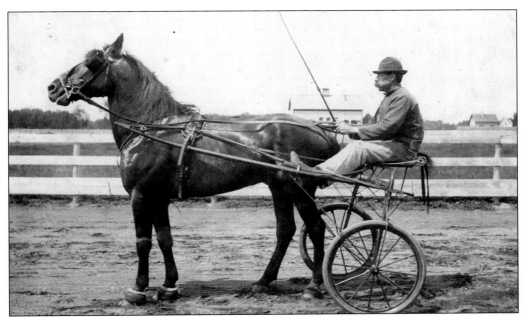

Most Mansfield residents would be surprised to learn that horseracing once took place right here in Mansfield. In 1869, the Mansfield Trotting Association organized "Mineral Spring Trotting Park" on the land where the Mansfield Airport now stands on Fruit Street. This photograph was snapped June 18, 1897, showing driver George Aird and J.W. Cobb's trotter, "Jack."

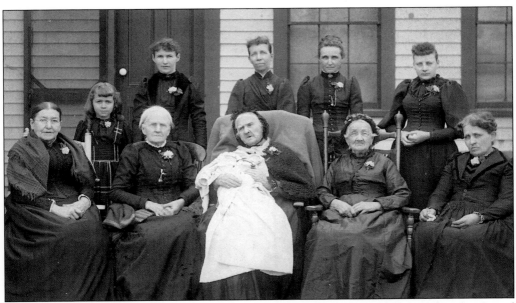

This fascinating 1893 photograph shows Mansfield women from 11 different decades. Listed from left to right are the following: (front row) Mrs. Margaret MacDonald, 70; Mrs. Mary Sherman, 80; Mrs. Betsy Davis, 100, holding Mina Treen, six weeks old; Mrs. Cynthia West, 90; and Miss Hepsibah Stearns, 60; (back row) Miss Bessie N. Dunbar, ten; Miss Alice M. Pratt, 30; Mrs. Edna M. Stearns, 50; Mrs. Carrie M. Perry, 40; and Miss Lillian Buck, 20.

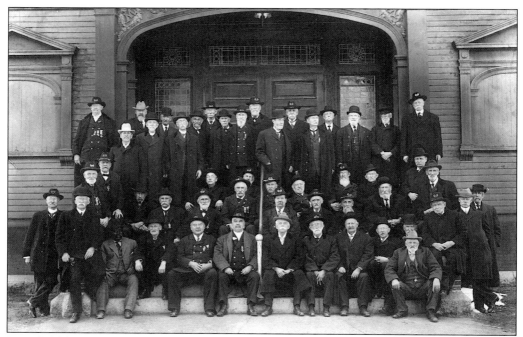

Mansfield has a proud record of serving the nation at wartime. During the Civil War, 261 Mansfield men answered the call. This photograph shows members of Mansfield's John Rogers Post of the GAR posing on the steps of Mansfield's old town hall.

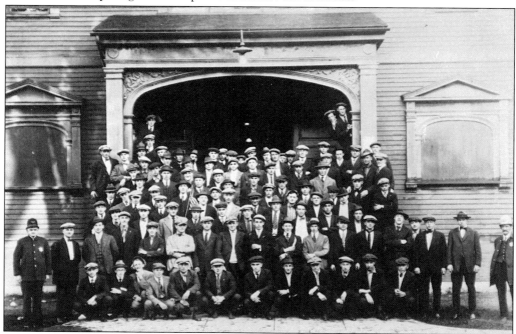

Some of Mansfield's 312 men who served in WW I strike the same pose as the Civil War veterans on the town hall steps. This photograph was probably taken soon after the war's end, and is possibly from the town's "Welcome Home" celebration for returning veterans in 1919.

Veterans Day 1956 was the setting of this photograph taken at the American Legion Hall on Fruit Street. Post Commander Norman A. Vickery, center, is seen congratulating Charles P. Crowd, left, and Donald Tucker Jr., right, on their receiving the gold-star life membership for service to the legion post. (Courtesy of *The Mansfield News*.)

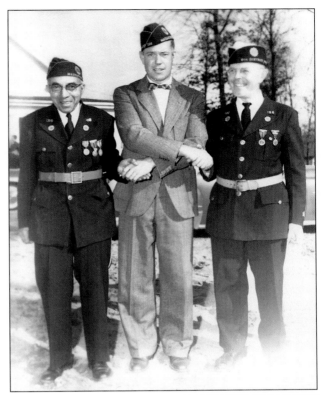

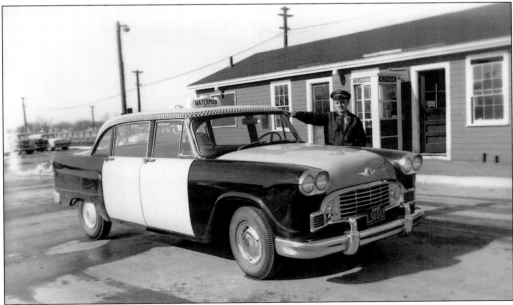

Waterman Taxi was another longtime Mansfield institution. Begun by the Waterman family, the cab company transported Mansfield residents for generations. Here a Waterman driver poses in the late 1950s in front of the Mansfield train station, ready for a fare. (Courtesy of *The Mansfield News*.)

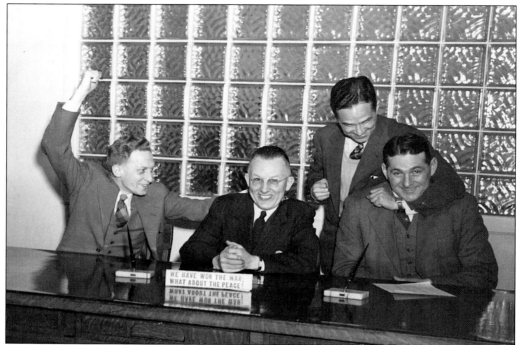

"We have won the war: What about the peace?" So reads the sign in front of the Mansfield Board of Selectmen during a lighthearted moment in January 1946. Pictured from left to right are: Everett Grant, Royal Patriquin, Town Manager James Shurtleff, and John Prescott. Missing from the photograph are Selectmen Schuyler Wellman and Frederick Hewey.

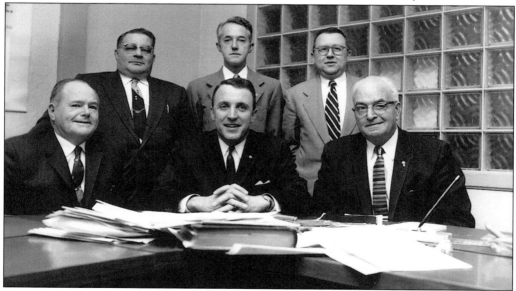

The board of selectmen struck a more serious pose in 1959. Pictured from left to right are the following: (front row) George Dustin, Chairman Orlando Souza, and Joseph Cataloni; (back row) Salvatore DeLutis, Edward Jameson, and Town Manager Paul Flynn. (Courtesy of *The Mansfield News*.)

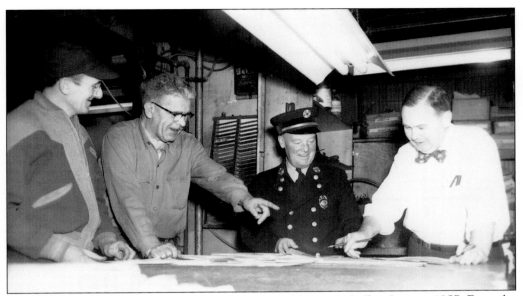

These four men are busy planning advertising for the Firemen's Ball in January 1957. From the left are firemen Arthur Alden and Hamilton Wallis, with Fire Chief Harry Davison. At the right is Howard Fowler, longtime editor of *The Mansfield News* who was both widely admired and widely disliked for his outspoken newspaper work. (Courtesy of *The Mansfield News*.)

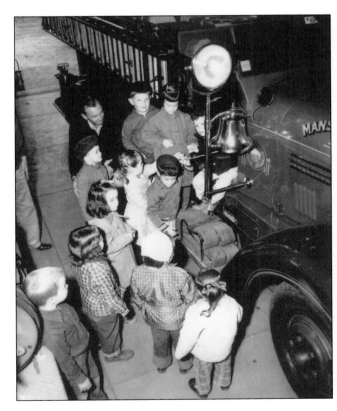

Firetrucks have long been a natural attraction for children, and this 1959 photograph is an example of that. Here we see future fire chief Cyril Bellavance showing schoolchildren the workings of the fire department apparatus. (Courtesy of *The Mansfield News*.)

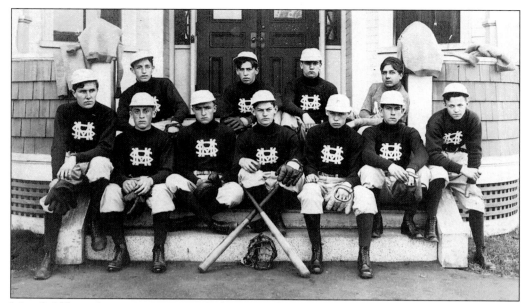

Mansfield has a long connection with the sport of baseball. As early as just a few years after the Civil War, Mansfield had a traveling town team. Here we see the 1906 Mansfield High School baseball team ready to take on an opposing nine.

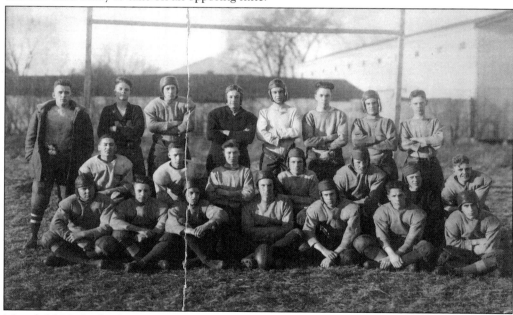

Mansfield High also has a proud football tradition. Here is the 1919 team posing at Fuller's Field, located at the end of Wilson Place. Pictured from left to right are the following: (first row) unidentified, George Jackson, Clair Jackson, Donald Pike, Clarence Morse, Kenneth Patterson, and David Sheehan; (second row) Carl DePrizio, Raymond Morse, Wilbur Johnson, James Lodico, Carl Anderson, Joseph Todesco, and Frank Bowers; (third row) Coach Sid Drew, Herman Barker, Rector Fullerton, Benton Winslow, Perle Strople, Norwood Robinson, Sheldon David, and Howard Fowler.

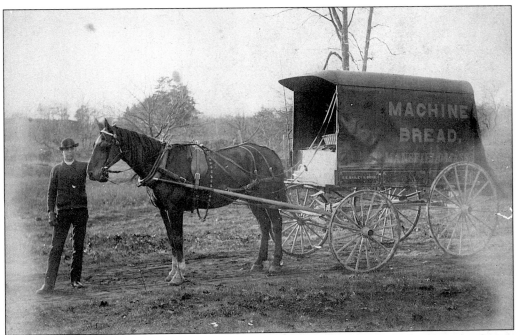

Located on School Street, the Bailey bakeshop opened in 1848 along the railroad tracks. Owner George E. Bailey contributed much to the baking profession, including the invention of a large pan for cooking crackers and perfecting the Bailey oven, which was widely used around the world. Fire claimed most of the shop in 1888, but Mr. Bailey continued in the oven business.

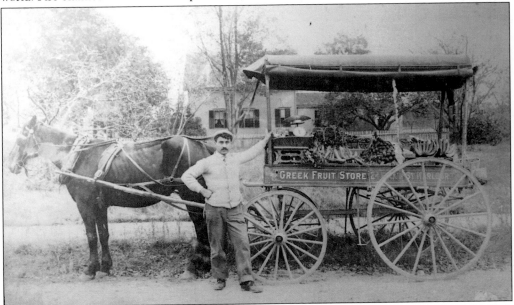

Theodore Penesis, a Greek immigrant, had several Mansfield businesses in the early 20th century. Here Mr. Penesis stops on Fruit Street and poses in front of his wagon. Mr. Penesis later owned a candy store and a restaurant in Mansfield, and eventually opened the well-known Chicken Coop restaurant in Norton.

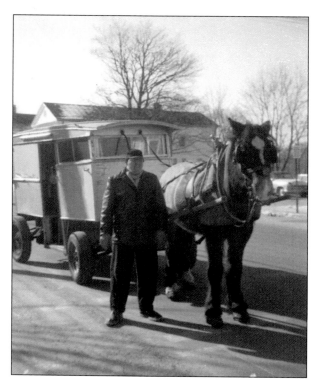

Milkman Kenny Fletcher became a Mansfield institution over the years. Still using his horse-drawn wagon long after others were using motorized trucks, Kenny delivered milk around town until the 1960s. An obliging fellow, Kenny enjoyed giving youngsters a ride on his milk wagon. Except for "the fresh ones," all the children would be given a piece of candy.

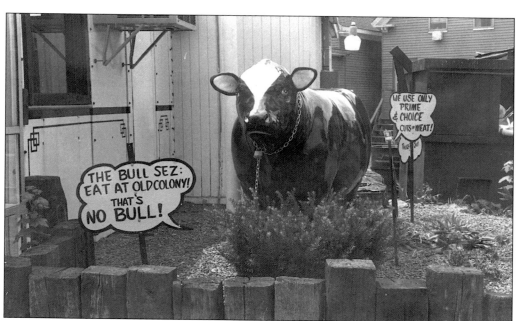

Our final photograph is another Mansfield memory that is now gone. The Old Colony Diner Bull stood next to the establishment for several years, and still brings a smile to those that remember it. The bull was removed permanently about ten years ago, but reminds us of the many people, places, and faces, some gone and some remaining, that have made Mansfield unique.